Cut Out the Losers

Lessons Learned

MJ Parker

**ISBN-13: 978-0692873557
(Grand Union Partners)**

ISBN-10:0692873554

Library of Congress Control Number: **2017941740**
LCCN Imprint Name: Grand Union Partners, NJ

DEDICATION

This book started out as a personal journal. It will make you laugh, it will make you cry, and it will horrify you all at the same time. It is dedicated to my loving husband, my one and only, the "lid" to my "pot." The book was started over twenty-five years ago but finished recently as a result of his constant pushing to publish it. If it weren't for him, it would never have been finished. I am eternally grateful to him. He has always maintained that the true stories and morals at the end are valuable lessons that could help others avoid some of the mistakes that I have made.

CONTENTS OF LOSERS

ACKNOWLEDGMENTS

All the losers in this book have helped me become a stronger person and to recognize "new" losers more readily, allowing me to cut them out sooner. The chapters in this book are based upon true stories in my life, outlining lessons I have learned, told from my own point of view. The book also outlines my stupidity in every case and why the loser should never have been trusted to begin with. All the names have been changed for privacy reasons.

My definition of losers? Self-absorbed people I have encountered in my life with their own agendas. They all wished to better their lives, use me, or hurt me with little or no concern about how it would affect me and/or my loved ones.

If these stories help even one person avoid a loser in his or her own life, then it will be worth the effort it took, to write this book.

1 MARK—KYLE'S LOSER BOYFRIEND

At one point in my life, I shared a house in Florida with five other people. The house-sharing experience started with my best friend, Kyle, who is gay. We soon found that the rent was much too high for just the two of us and the house was much bigger than we needed. So we began one of many roommate searches.

Sometime during this search, we met Mark at El Goya, one of our favorite gay bars in Tampa, Florida. It was an urban setting, fun, and exciting. It contained mostly Cuban restaurants, shops, and housing smack in the heart of Ybor City. The bar is no longer there, but it was the best for miles around. It had five smaller bars situated within: a country-western bar, a pool room, a conversation bar, a large disco, and a show bar. We had loads of drag-queen friends who starred in the show, and we went to see them grace the stage as we drank our faces off. Many of them were quite beautiful, and all of them were talented. The shows were excellent, and the audiences were always diverse. Everyone loved the shows.

We had a couple of really good fun-loving years in that bar, and it was nice for me because it was filled mostly with gay people and I could relax, let my hair down, and have a good time without having to play the dating game. We grew close to most of the entertainers and often had them over to our home. Our neighbors just loved seeing six-foot-tall, Amazon-like "women" adorned with glitter and makeup sauntering up our driveway. In today's world, I don't think anyone would look twice, but at the time it was a bit on the unusual side. I think the neighbors might have been afraid, though, because they never spoke to us. Then again, it could be our three large Dobermans that patrolled our yard constantly. Some folks are just not dog people.

It was Kyle who met Mark first. Kyle was struck instantly as if he were hit by a bolt of lightning. Mark was short and had dark hair and strikingly beautiful blue eyes, which was the top draw for Kyle. Mark was a fabulous hairdresser who gave us different colors and styles fit for the red carpet. He did the hair of our entertainer friends, and everyone was impressed with his skills. Within a few months, Kyle and I adored him.

At first, Mark and Kyle would just meet up at the bar, but soon, we would go to dinner with him, have him over for evenings, and go shopping and to movies. For once, we found a friend who was willing to pay his share instead of mooching off us all the time. We genuinely liked him. Kyle was falling deeply in love and spoke to me about having Mark move in with us. I was excited by the thought of having a full-time hairdresser in our home as well as getting an additional roommate so we could all save on rent. The night Kyle asked Mark to move in, we all had a nice dinner and drinks to celebrate. The five inhabitants were now Kyle, our friend Jeff, his boyfriend Ralph, Mark, and I.

It's funny how your adoration of some people can fade when you live with them. Within weeks, you begin to realize you have made a mistake and wonder how you will survive the next eleven months on the lease. At first, it was little things. Mark had a temper, but I chalked it up to his tendency to be a clean freak who would let loose with screaming fits every time he found a fingerprint, anywhere. He was grouchy all the time. Mark was gifted because he was able to hide the fact that he was a loser.

We soon found out that Mark also had a past, which would affect our lives as we knew them. He had a deep secret. Mark was still married to a straight woman. How could someone so obviously gay snare and reel in a straight woman? He claimed to be in the "process of divorce," and we had no reason not to believe him. A bigger secret was that Mark had a set of triplets, all boys aged three. We had no idea when Mark saw the kids over the first few months, but he certainly hid this fact well.

One night, Mark got Kyle all liquored up and confessed. This would now mean that the boys would visit our house every weekend from Friday night until Sunday night. Although the boys were adorable, they were not conducive to a house full of people aged twenty-one to twenty-five whose mission was to drink, dance, eat, and sleep all weekend, every weekend. Our weekend party habits quickly came to a halt, and Kyle ended up in the kitchen on Saturday and Sundays, wearing an apron and cooking. It was frustrating to watch my party-animal friend turn into a housewife at such a young age.

Mark was a candle freak and had dozens of them glowing all over the house. He spent a fortune on candles and came home with new ones when he went shopping or on a trip. This was nice because the house always smelled good and our expensive electric bill was cut back a few bucks.

Mark's arrival also included two large parrots that talked nonstop and cursed like sailors. He specifically told everyone in the house *not* to let them out of their cages because it was nearly impossible to get them back in. He mentioned that the birds didn't like anyone except for him and we should expect that they would bite. The birds did not seem aggressive, and Mark had a tendency to exaggerate, so I didn't believe him. Being an animal person, I assumed I could handle a couple of big birds and get them into their cages when necessary. Naturally, the moment Mark left for the first time, we let the birds out of their cages to fly freely in the house.

Who knew that Mark was telling the truth? The birds swooped through the air, screeching and swearing loudly enough for the entire development and surrounding neighborhoods to hear. It sounded like we lived in an Amazon rain forest. They must have been nervous because they were letting poop loose as they flew, and it was getting all over the living room. In their travels, their wings went through some of the candles and the end feathers became singed and covered in candle wax.

When we tried to coax the parrots back into the cage, they snapped and clawed and squawked at us. This time, Mark was not lying: they really did not like us. We ran into the kitchen, which cut us off from the rest of the house. The birds were still screeching at an ear-piercing level, and we were afraid to go into the living room. Instead, we stayed in the kitchen—Kyle in his apron and me in my pajamas, peeking around the corner and counting the moments until Mark arrived home.

Mark was whistling and rattling his keys down the walk when he arrived, obviously in a good mood. Kyle and I smiled at each other in the kitchen, thinking things would be okay. He was in a good mood, thank goodness. However, once Mark got inside and the birds saw him, they started screaming and swearing as if to tell their "side" to Mark. The real shock was that one of them spoke my name. Gawd, they were smart. What little tattletales. Mark was absolutely furious. His birds were nervous and covered in candle wax, but he was upset more than anything else that we didn't obey his orders. It was clear how the birds learned to swear so well.

Mark and the birds were screaming and swearing the whole time he was trying to get them back into their cage. I was surprised that Mark had such a bad temper over something that in the grand scheme of things was not that big of a deal. At first we were afraid of the birds; now we were scared of living with Mark—exorcist boy. It took him at least an hour to get the birds back into their cage. We had headaches from all the screaming and screeching. Kyle and I let out sighs of relief when the little bastards were finally locked up again. Mark wouldn't speak to us the rest of the day and night, but we didn't care. We had been hiding in the kitchen from those birds for so long, and I really had to pee. We could finally get to our bathroom, the bedrooms, and the front door now that the birds were back under lock and key.

The next morning while I was getting ready for work, I went into the kitchen for coffee and to collect the lunch that Kyle always made me. I was in shock when he turned to hand me the coffee. He had two black eyes. He held his finger to his lips as a signal to shush so I would not rile Mark, who was sitting in the bathroom having a crap with the door open, next to the living room. He could have heard anything we were saying from his proximity. Mark always had his bathroom moments with the door wide open so he didn't miss a thing. He disgusted all of us, but we just got used to it after a while. I figured out quickly that I didn't want things to get insane, so I loudly asked Kyle to help me carry some stuff to my car so I could leave for work. As we hit the front door, I heard the toilet flush and the sink water running. But Kyle was able to quickly tell me that Mark beat him up over the bird incident and he was now afraid of Mark.

Needless to say, we couldn't live in the house with a psychopath. I asked Kyle to come to work with me so we could figure out what to do. Kyle said no and told me he would work it out himself.

When I arrived home that evening, Kyle and Mark were on the couch sitting lovey-dovey, holding hands, and asking about my day. I couldn't believe it. I thought Kyle had gone mental. Turns out Mark filled his ears with a load of crap, claiming never to do it again, yada, yada, yada. From my angle, I couldn't even see Kyle's eyeballs because of the blackness around them. It wasn't until his eyes darted to the side that I could make out a bit of white.

It took about five more beatings before Kyle admitted he was a battered boyfriend. The other residents and I had a family meeting and told Mark he would have to leave and that Kyle wanted nothing more to do with him. We were kind enough to pack his things while he was at work and notified him that his belongings—including his bastard birds—were in the garage.

Surprisingly, Mark went peacefully without any help from law enforcement. Kyle, me and our roommates went back to our partying, but months went by before we could get Kyle to relax at any bars. Kyle was worried about seeing Mark. Turns out he had nothing to fear because Mark never did come to our neck of the woods again. We had been successful in cutting the loser out of our lives forever.

The Moral: You never know anyone until you live with them. If someone abuses you once, it's their fault. After that, it's your fault for staying with that person and putting up with it.

2 LOLA–THE LOSER LANDLORD

Kyle and I hated all people by now. The list of former roommates and all their issues was so long that I could have written a book on them alone. Still, it was now behind us and we were ready for our next plan. Our goal was to find and rent a small, affordable house with a yard for the dogs and absolutely no roommates ever again. We dreamed of coming and going as we pleased, living in peace and harmony, and being able to pay for everything by ourselves.

Kyle and I began the search for a home and answered an advertisement that sounded too good to be true. We arrived at a sunny little neighborhood known as Cypress. It was a little farther out of Tampa than we would have liked, but still, just outside of Tampa. It was perfect. It had two bedrooms, two bathrooms, a little kitchen, a dining area, and a living room. There was a garage, and, best of all, a huge backyard that seemed to stretch into the sunset.

Lola was the landlord. She was weird looking with bleached-blond hair, white four-inch fingernails, tan skin like a brown shoe, and two-inch-thick makeup accented with heavy blue eye shadow. Kyle wasn't even paying attention as she took us through the house because he was busy pointing out her cosmetic flaws and fashion faux pas. She was short, but her hair was teased up enough to reach my five-foot-ten-inch height.

She took us around room by room and bragged on and on about the house and how each room was a dream. She also told us the monthly rental cost, which was about $250 less than any other place we had looked at. Kyle and I looked across the room at each other, trying to see over her hair. We had a conversation with our eyes. We were both thinking, *Wow, this woman is really behind the times, probably doesn't even know she is not charging enough.*

We told Lola we wanted the place and asked when we could move in. She made arrangements for us to meet her at the house the next day with the key. She said we could move in right away. We still had two weeks left on our lease at the other house, but the sooner we could get into our new place and start fresh, the better. We went home to pack.

We were really excited the next day. We brought the three Dobermans with us, and they romped around the yard while we unpacked and set up house. We drew straws for the room with the bathroom, and Kyle won. This didn't matter much to me; the other bathroom was directly across from my room. Lola's decor choices were as horrible as her fashion statements, so we were drawing straws to sleep in the atomic-blue room versus the puke-green room. Who cared? We were free of roommates once and for all.

We were exhausted. Packing and moving all day takes a toll, and since all our stuff was at the new house, we decided to sleep there. We just took to our rooms and crashed.

We had both taken off a few days from work. Kyle worked as a German dancer at a popular adventure theme park. I worked as an office administrator for a hair-replacement clinic and was considered the "technical wizard" there. When I think about the so-called computer I used, with a matching daisy matrix printer the size of a room, it makes me laugh. Both of us were completely sick of our jobs and made a vow to get new ones after we settled in.

Part of Kyle's job was to get decked out in lederhosen shorts and offer his hand to female guests of the theme park so they could dance with him. He got so sick of the people that he felt like punching them instead of dancing with them. On occasion, I would go to the park and sit through his German show all day so he could choose me out of the audience to dance with. We would whirl around the wooden dance arena together as he spoke under his breath about the "tourists" I saved him from. What are friends for, after all?

In my job at the white-trash hair-replacement clinic, I was tired of men coming into our place with their hair in paper bags and waiting in the lobby where I sat. They were always interrupting my work, telling me their "bald" stories and talking about the difference the hair made in their lives. Our hairdresser would wash and style their wigs and then sew them back onto their heads. I was so busy and all the stories sounded alike by now. They really needed to hire a receptionist, but were too cheap to do so. All of the clients' hair looked like cotton after so many times in a hot dryer and being stuffed into a bag. Every one of those men looked so much better bald.

The owner was an old man trying to appear young, and wore polyester pants and golf shirts, and always had his overly large belt buckle on. His permanent dark tan added to the ensemble. He screeched into the parking lot every day in his red Corvette. His reserved spot was right in front of the door, so I witnessed this each and every day, several times a day. The only thing that changed was the color of his daily golf shirt. I placed mental "bets" in my head, trying to guess the "color of the day". He and our hairdresser, Becky, would lock themselves in his office for hours claiming to work.

Becky, the hairdresser, was a trashy, sluttish-looking girl who dressed in clothes two sizes too small so she could show off her body. She smoked long skinny brown cigarettes and always had one in her hands. Her nails were too thick and too long to be real and I had no idea how she styled hair with them. I often wondered how she wiped herself in the bathroom. She thought she was hot shit and never spoke more than a word or two to me. That actually worked out for both of us, because I had nothing in common with her and didn't want to get involved in her life. She would get the men in her chair and while she was sewing their hair on, she would put her boobs in their faces. She was always bragging about how this brought her the best tips.

She still found time for rides in the owner's Corvette, long lunches, talks in the parking lot, and, of course, hours alone with him in his office. It was funny to watch them drive up in the convertible. I often thought that Becky did a good job sewing his hair on because his wig never blew off and wasn't even disheveled with the amount of goop she put on it. Then again, Becky would be right there on the spot to fix it if it had. At one point, he made a television commercial that should have been called "What *Not* to Do in Business." They filmed him driving up with Becky in the Corvette, showing how his hair stayed on even in the wind. Overall, I cared little about what they did. They were always gone or locked in the office. I could do whatever I wanted. I needed Becky only when the men and their hair showed up.

Bottom line, we both had stupid jobs and we couldn't wait to dump them. But with this new house, we felt renewed. We told each other we could spend our days off looking for new jobs, and life was good overall. We were definitely in a better position than ever before because it was just us in the house without any roommates. The fact that we always had each other was the biggest comfort of all.

During our time off, we laid our shelf paper, cleaned everything to a shine, and made our new house a home. In addition, we had to go back and clean the other house in order to get our security deposit refund, which never happened.

We lived in the house for about two weeks, and at first, everything was going well. Then, overnight things turned to crap.

The heavens opened up, and it rained. It rained and rained and rained. It rained from Friday morning until Sunday morning. During this time, we didn't even feel like going out. We hung around in the living room watching television and eating and drinking.

All of a sudden, Kyle looked down and started screaming. "What in the *hell* is that?" I followed his finger with my eyes, and as Kyle jumped up onto a chair, I noticed a large scorpion on the kitchen floor. We were scared to death.

Kyle got the thing into a jar so we could show it to Lola. Being the landlord, she would most definitely have to get an exterminator out to fix this. There was no way we would sleep soundly in that house until she did. Day after day, we were finding scorpions everywhere. They were in our sinks, our toilets, our beds, and the couch. We yelled at the dogs constantly not to chew them. Later on, we heard that Florida scorpions had no venom. Who wanted to find out? All we knew was that they didn't like rain and planted themselves in our house to get away from it. And venom or not, we both had received painful bites from them.

We took turns calling Lola about the scorpions over and over every single day. Being naive, we thought, *You bitch! You are never home.* Both so stupid, not realizing she was probably at home, listening to the phone ring, putting another coat of makeup on her face, looking like she had visited a mortician. In those days, we had no cell phones and most people didn't regularly use answering machines. We were at Lola's mercy.

One morning after a horrible rainstorm, things got progressively worse.

I opened the back door to let the dogs out at the first sign of sun, but as I stood at the door with them fighting behind me to get out, I noticed large piles of something brown on the back lawn. At first I was irritated thinking someone had let their cow loose in our yard. We had only two neighbors in the entire area. The one to the left of us always put her baby outside in a playpen by itself. The neighbor on the right side was a single guy who we barely saw. Neither neighbor had a cow, so I had no clue why we had huge piles of shit in the yard. What wild animal was big enough to leave those, I thought?

Suddenly, I noticed one of the piles moving. As I stepped through the door, it dawned on me that the piles were all alive. It was like some nightmare that comes to you slowly. The piles closest to me began to draw back, and I realized I was viewing a yard full of snakes. I have never been afraid of snakes; in fact, I have owned various snakes as pets. But this was Florida. Everyone knows that Florida snakes are usually venomous. I quickly shut the door and ran to wake up Kyle.

As we sat at the window and stared out, we were speaking to each other at the same time. "How many of them do you think there are?" "What kind do you think they are?" "Oh my God, can you imagine what would have happened if we let the dogs out?" Kyle went to the back door to take a closer look. After all, Lola wouldn't purposely rent a place to someone knowing there were dangerous, venomous snakes in the yard. Then we began to think about the $250 cut in rent. And we began to think about how quickly she let us move in. No credit checks, no employment checks, and she wanted all her money in cash.

As I held the dogs, Kyle stepped onto the back stairs. Two of the brown piles drew back and opened their mouths. Kyle saw white. We had approximately eighty to one hundred cottonmouth snakes in our yard. Kyle quickly jumped inside and slammed the door behind him.

We went out the front to the neighbor next door to see if she knew anything. As we left our front door, we remembered that she kept her infant in the playpen outside all the time. It was unlikely she knew about the snakes. She wasn't home. We would have to come back.

All day and all night, we called Lola. Still no answer. Next, we began calling our parents.

Kyle's mother, who lived in Tampa, went berserk and told us that between the scorpions and cottonmouths, someone would be sure to die. I was thinking how positive she always was and how uplifted I felt after speaking to her (sarcasm). Kyle asked if we could move to her house until we could reach Lola. There was a resounding "no" down the phone. My, she had been a big help, I thought (sarcasm).

Kyle's mother was a nagging, overbearing, critical woman who needed to be in our business for everything. Yet she was never there to help us with anything important. He is lucky he is gay because no daughter-in-law could ever have pleased her. She also had the largest nostrils I have ever seen on a human. It was impossible to pay attention to anything she said because her nostrils drew me in like a train wreck.

My parents were in New York City, so there was no way we were moving that far away, but I called anyway. My parents have always been the true voice of reason, and I knew they would have some advice to impart upon us. Kyle, who was ghostly scared by now, sat next to me. I was sick to my stomach as I dialed up my parents.

Both of my parents answered the phone as usual, each on an extension. I blurted out our latest troubles to them. In hindsight, I think that my life truly entertained them. My brother always stuck to the script, and they were always proud of him. He had goals, he followed them, and he was successful. I, on the other hand, had a way to raise their blood pressures instantaneously. At least they had something to talk about when my name came up. They were sincerely proud of me too; I just pictured conversations with them being much different from those they had with my brother. Kyle sat next to me interjecting and shouting forgotten items into the story. First, my father offered his advice. As he began, I thought, *Good old Dad. Always knows what to do. Contact a lawyer? Call the housing authority? Maybe even he would get in on the action and make some calls and Lola would be really sorry she messed with us.*

My father's advice (rest his soul) was something I shall never forget to my dying day.

He told me about this documentary he once watched on television about pigs. Apparently, when pitted with snakes in a battle, the pigs would always win because of their razor-sharp teeth. I sat quietly trying to take in what the man was saying. "Razor-sharp teeth?" I said. "Yes!" said my Dad. "What you really need to do is go out and get two pigs. They will make short work of those snakes for you." I sat in disbelief for a couple of seconds, and Kyle was prompting me. "What is it? What are they saying? What about razor-sharp teeth?" I put my finger to my lips to shush him and asked my father, "Are you serious? Let's pretend that I even *remotely* knew where to get two pigs with razor-sharp teeth, but that is the most ridiculous thing I have ever heard." "I don't know how to take care of pigs!"

My mother chimed in. "Joe, that is the most ludicrous thing I have ever heard." I thought to myself, *Finally, someone with sense is about to speak*. My mother followed up with her exceptional advice. "She would need a permit for those pigs."

It was at that moment I realized that there was simply no help for our situation. We were living in hell because of a horrible landlady who obviously knew our plight and rented the house cheap to get any sucker in there to pay the rent. We were the current suckers.

During the next three weeks, we called and called and called her. We had no idea where she lived, we had no idea of her last name, and we had no address for her on any paper, because we only signed one that we could recall. That was a generic lease agreement, with most of the stuff scratched out on it. We were dumbfounded and had no idea what to do.

We did call the police, the SPCA, and the Florida Game Commission. The commission came out and told us that we lived right on swampland. He explained that everything would be fine on sunny days, but when the rain season began, we would be in big trouble. He explained that gators and crocs would more than likely join their little cottonmouth friends and our dogs should never be put outside, ever.

We did eventually get to the woman next door with the baby in the playpen. Of course when she opened the door, we realized she spoke no English. Kyle had some high school Spanish, but he didn't know any of the important words like "pig, cottonmouth or scorpion". We did our part for her and told the guy from the Florida Game Commission that someone needed to warn her. We explained about her baby in the playpen. I have no idea what happened to those neighbors because they remained in that house after we had gone from ours. Kyle and I were screwed. We began to call Lola like crazy people trying to reach out to her to refund our rent money, as we knew we had no choice but to get out.

We lived in "cottonmouth city" for another two months while we saved money to move into a swamp-free house. We had to walk the dogs on leashes four times a day in the neighborhood, because we couldn't put them out in the yard. We never heard from Lola again, and therefore she never refunded any money to us.

We moved into a home in Temple Terrace (outskirts of Tampa, once again) to begin another chapter of fun.

The Moral: If something seems too good to be true, it probably is.

Side Note: After a few months went by, Kyle's mother called to see if we had read the paper. We had not, and asked her why. She asked us to use the speaker phone and read a front-page story to us. It was all about the police finding Lola's body chopped up in little pieces in some white-trash sleazy motel.

Second Moral: What goes around comes back around.

3 VICTOR–THE CONNIVING LOSER

To this day, Victor remains one of the weirdest people I have ever known.

As with most people, the initial contact with Victor was fine. We happened to be out one evening at another favorite gay bar called The Plantation. This place served up twenty-five-cent screwdrivers every Tuesday evening from seven to nine o'clock. Although Tuesday is not a typical party night, this place was jammed because of the nearly free alcohol. In those days, the drunken-driving laws were nonexistent. Everyone would head to the bar, tank up, dance, chat, and drive home to prepare for a long Wednesday workday. It was something I would not dream of doing and neither did Kyle. We were no angels, but we were very responsible about driving and neither would ever drive drunk. In addition, there was barely any parking to be had, so we would carpool with friends or take taxis or a bus. We learned the secret of taking Alka-Seltzer before bed after drinking, so we could wake up perky for work the next day. I think we were personally responsible for their jumping stock in those days.

Florida bars typically have outside areas meant for chatting up and relaxing. Some had discos, which delivered pounding beats for dancing. It was under the disco ball where Kyle and I first met Victor. During *Rock Lobster*, Victor just appeared with one huge jump between Kyle and me. We had no idea if he was gay or straight because he continued to dance with both of us, and we didn't care anyway.

Tuesday after Tuesday, Victor came to the bar and danced with us. Never saying a word, but instead just springing in and out of our dances. He was harmless, he danced well, and we just got used to him.

We had been talking about having a lavish party to celebrate our birthdays, holidays and anything else that would take place that year, all at once. We printed up fliers in order to invite people and passed them around the various bars we "haunted". On the night of the party, there was a knock at the door and when I opened it, there was Victor.

I am a horrible judge of age, but with his black-and-gray hair and the structure of his face, I placed him at around thirty-five years old. Quite a contrast to our household, where the age averaged twenty-three. Victor had a medium build, nothing notable or special, and he was dressed in khakis and a button-down shirt every time we saw him. I don't think Victor owned any dress-down clothing; he wasn't the type. He stayed at the party but didn't mingle a bit. Instead, he just sat in the kitchen and watched us scurry about performing host duties. He wasn't in the way, but it was weird. We still wondered if Victor was interested in either Kyle or me because he said nothing—just had an empty stare. The successful party ended, and many people—as was customary—ended up crashing on our floors and couches. We had a tremendous mess to clean, but we went to bed anyway. When we awoke, Victor was one of the bodies left behind. Victor was asleep on the kitchen floor, pretty much where we left him.

He just would not leave. Neither Kyle nor I have ever been known to be subtle, so I came right out and asked him when he was planning on going home. He said he hadn't planned anything and never did plan anything. Not an answer, but since he didn't appear to want to leave, we figured he could help us clean up. And clean he did. He jumped right in with the rest of us, and in about five hours the house showed no signs of having 150 drunken people from the night before. We were pleasantly surprised for all the help he gave us and we thanked Victor and invited him to dinner.

During dinner, we tried to engage him in conversation. He was strange with evasive and sarcastic answers to our questions. To me, he seemed immature or maybe crazy—who knew at this point? He proclaimed to be "sort of" an alcoholic. We didn't think anything of that. After all, we were drinking like alcoholics at that stage of our lives. Victor claimed he did not work and didn't have to. We heard a story about his mother and father passing away, and he claimed he didn't know how they died. Something else surprising was that he lived on the next street, in our development, within walking distance of our house. It was odd that we had never crossed paths, since we walked our large dogs all the time around the entire neighborhood. Then again, if he had seen us, he probably did so from behind a curtain in his home. We came out and asked if he was gay or straight, and he simply said, "Yes." I did not see any place for him in the boyfriend area of my life, but he seemed harmless enough. We continued to invite him to game nights, parties, and dinners at our home. We never once went to his home for anything.

One day, I was walking the dogs by myself. As I approached Victor's street, he was getting out of his car and heading toward his house. I felt better having validated at least one story he told. He did live on this street. He seemed different on this day somehow—more together, more forthcoming with chitter-chatter, and quite obviously flirting with me. It was during this conversation that Victor asked me out on a date. Honestly, I didn't care for him in that sense, but it was like being drawn into a mystery novel. He was incredibly friendly and nice, and I assumed that I must have misjudged him through the year we had known him. After all, I had seen him only in social situations where he had been drinking alcohol or taking drugs. This was the first time I had encountered Victor alone, and in the daytime. The date was set. We were going to dinner and a movie. I went on with my walk and noted that Victor jumped back into his car and drove away. *I must have been mistaken. He wasn't coming home; he must have been leaving*, I thought.

During dinner, we got into a conversation about death and dying. He spoke about his parents, finally talking about how they had perished in an car accident. He cried bitterly and loudly. The entire restaurant was staring at times, but I didn't care. I have never been one to give a shit what people think. It was nice to see a more human side to Victor, and to hell with the onlookers. It was sad, and I felt sick for him. I thought to myself, *This is why Victor is such a weirdo*. Once Victor started talking, the floodgates opened wide. He never shut up the entire time and just went on and on and on. He then talked about how the movie might stop the "energy flow" we had going on and asked if I would like to come over and see pictures of his parents and his childhood. I did not want to subject myself to more of this behavior, but I felt like a Good Samaritan and agreed to go with him. We lived so close to him that I figured everything would be fine. I didn't call home to speak to Kyle because he knew I had left with Victor, and I had no reason to worry.

Victor and I walked into his home at approximately 8:00 p.m. The outside of the house appeared to be average, so it was with great shock that I entered a huge, lavishly decorated foyer. The home had white sparkly ceilings, and the further we walked, the more the house unfolded. It was the stretch limousine of real estate. The home was spectacular and pristine. You could certainly eat off any floor you wished to. Everything was bright white with slight accents of green, detailed to perfection. I could not stop looking at this stunning house. It became immediately evident that Victor was filthy rich and a clean freak, both startling contrasts to my first impressions of him. It seemed that knowing Victor in the day, was completely different from knowing Victor in a crowded bar. I was now intrigued by this man. Although money has never been a huge reason for me to date anyone, I was struck by his wealth. I didn't want to date him, I just wanted to question him. I wanted to know how he received and maintained his fortune and assumed that his parents had left it to him. I thought how sad it was however. A double-edged sword: having all that money but also having both parents dead. I would never want that kind of wealth.

Victor asked to be excused. Within a few minutes, he shouted out, "Hey, you have to come in and see this. You will love it." I followed the voice down the hall and poked my head around the corner of a room. Nothing could prepare me for what I was about to see.

In the middle of a gorgeous cathedral-ceilinged room completely surrounded with mirrors stood Victor, stark naked except for socks and shoes. In a contest for hairiest man ever, he would win hands down. I truly thought he was wearing a long sweater at first. In his hand was a hairbrush. In the middle of the floor was a chair.

I was frozen in shock.

He told me not to worry and said he realized that this might look weird to me. He then spoke softly yet deliberately in almost a scared manner. The words spilled out: "Would you please spank and beat me? You could sit in the chair and I could lie across your lap like the bad child I am, and you can beat me until I bleed or bruise really bad." I began slowly backing up toward the door, and words just bubbled from his lips. "It's not what you think. I am not a big weirdo." Needless to say, I was not sticking around to find out. I snaked my way out of that house faster than the roadrunner.

When I reached the front door, I flung it open and ran out of that house, around the fence, and down the street to my house. I was screaming "Help" the entire time to get anyone's attention possible. When I ran through the front door of our house at top speed, I surprised Kyle and he screamed. As I was loudly and hysterically telling the story, some of our friends who were over gathered around with wild-eyed looks. It took me quite a while to get the story out. They were interjecting questions and statements with "I knew it" looks on their faces. Our "inner circle" knew Victor and all agreed that he was strange.

Still, I wanted someone to speak to Victor and tell him he was no longer allowed in our home and not to feel welcome. It would just be too weird. I wanted to call the police, but the boys assured me that wanting to be spanked in your own home was not a crime.

Kyle and Jeff promised that they would go speak to Victor, but they would wait to see if he came over to our house. They would greet him at the front door and speak to him, not allowing him in. They explained that they didn't want him to answer the door with a gun or something because he was so strange.

In the meantime, the police came to our door and asked if a girl fitting my description lived there. I went to the door, and they asked me to step out and answer some questions. I was thrilled to see them, and didn't even stop to wonder why they had come. They were investigating a breaking-and-entering charge. *Did Victor call them because he was mad that I ran out? Was he afraid that I would tell people about him?* I started talking and answering questions and told them everything I knew.

They asked if I would come down to the station and repeat everything to help them fill out their crime report. The police explained that the neighbors had seen people coming and going out of this house for months and that the owners of the home were "snowbirds" who lived there only a few months out of the year. The neighbors had heard my screaming and saw me running out of the house and called the police. They pointed out to the police the house they had seen me run into.

At the end of it all, it turned out that Victor didn't even live in that house or that neighborhood at all. The police believed what I told them. (Who could make it up?) They decided not to charge me with breaking and entering into that home.

Instead, they asked me for any help I could give them. I cooperated fully, but I did not have many details because Victor had not shared much with us. I was able to give them his description and a description of his car. That was pretty much it.

Eventually, they caught up with Victor. The big dope had been stupid enough to leave his driver's license in that house and, as it turned out, the information on it was current and correct. They went to his residence and arrested him. Surprisingly, his parents were very much alive and he was living with them.

Everything he had told us was bullshit. He was obviously emotionally disturbed.

In Florida, they don't mess around. Victor went to prison for two years for breaking and entering. How Victor found the empty home in the first place has never been made known to me. But I thanked my lucky stars that the ending was not more tragic for me.

The Moral: If you have a negative gut impression of someone, you are usually correct. Don't go to an acquaintance's home unless someone knows you are there. In hindsight, I would say this is true, even if they *do* own the house.

4 VIRGINIA–THE ACADEMY AWARD LOSER

Looking back and comparing Virginia to the other loser/liars I have known, without a doubt if there were some kind of academy award for lying, Virginia would win hands down. It was my youth and lack of experience that masked Virginia's extraordinary talent for lying. I can only blame myself for getting caught up in the fabulous life she made up. Then again, Kyle was also taken in by her. Somehow that makes it all better as I reminisce over my stupidity.

Kyle and I met Virginia at one of the gay bars because she cozied up to us while the DJ was playing *It's Raining Men*. We enjoyed dancing and singing this song loudly along with the rest of the bar. Whenever the intro started playing, everyone screamed and packed the dance floor because it was a favorite in the eighties. And, along with the rest of the bar, there was Virginia.

She was very short. She had blond hair with a choppy man-like cut and was dressed like a man. It never occurred to me that she might be a lesbian. How could I have missed that? Then again, it did not occur to Kyle either. We continued to dance, and she stuck to us like glue for the rest of the night. Naturally, we shared our bar schedule with her. Soon she was showing up at every bar on the same nights we were there. Kyle and I didn't mind at first, but we got sick of her after about two months. We enjoyed each other's company and wanted to gossip and chat and be together. We didn't like our "stalker" at all. About the fourth time she came through the door, Kyle and I headed to another part of the bar to avoid her. No such luck. Poof, there she was every time we danced. We both started to be rather cold to her and even exchanged words with her that would stop anyone from coming back for more. Not Virginia. She was like mold that just kept growing back after a harsh scrubbing. We simply could not rid ourselves of her.

We changed our nightlife schedule a bit in order to avoid her. It did work for a while, but then we had a party at our house and, of course, someone brought Virginia. We gave up. She was everywhere, and she would continue to be everywhere. Kyle and I just shrugged at each other and figured she was now part of our lives. We thought she was harmless enough and definitely a lonely little thing, so we let her stay.

In those days, almost all parties were overnights. Nobody left. This was good because we didn't want anyone drinking and driving. They would come, get drunk, and pass out all over the house. The parties would take place at different houses each time, and through the years everyone just woke up on a Sunday morning to a sea of bodies all over the house. It was a totally natural thing for all of us. We just walked over the people as we got on with our day and eventually they would leave. If we were lucky, people helped clean up the mess, and we were fortunate to have lots of friends like that. On this particular occasion, Virginia was one of those cleaners.

After we got everything cleaned up, only Kyle, Virginia, and I remained, and we decided to go get something to eat. Tampa, Florida, has many little places to grab a cheap bite; however, Virginia told us to get dressed up. She was taking us to a famous steak house in Tampa called "Berns". This was an establishment that cost megabucks. She claimed that we had been so nice to her and she wanted to treat us after all we had done. It took no time at all for Kyle and me to run upstairs and get ready. Within an hour, we were sitting at this fabulous, overpriced restaurant, drinking wine and eating appetizers. We also began a conversation with Virginia in order to learn more about her and to see if we could establish a sort of wavelength with her.

Virginia's life sounded nothing short of awesome. She lived in a "castle" in Tampa's Bay Harbor area. She could afford this because she was an attorney. Also, her parents had both passed away and left her a wealthy woman. We were not impressed with material things, but this woman and her wealth wowed us because neither of us had ever known any "real" person with so much money. She asked Kyle and me what we were doing the next weekend. She was offering a weekend in Miami, all expenses paid. She claimed to have a case that she needed to finish up and offered to get us our own room. She explained that Kyle and I could go to South Beach for the day, and when she was done, she would join us for a party that we would never forget. We told her we had very little money and could not afford to pay her back. She swiped her hand in the air and told us it was her pleasure to treat us. She claimed that she would relish our company during the four or so hours it would take to drive from Tampa to Miami. We agreed and shook hands on it. We then went our separate ways, and Kyle and I chatted about it all the way home. Since we would have no expenses, we were going shopping for a new bathing suit each and would stock up at the liquor store for our hotel room. We spent the entire week planning our trip to Miami.

On Wednesday night of that week, I came home to a strange situation. Kyle was pacing back and forth in front of our house, and Virginia was standing on the walkway behind him smoking. The last I had spoken to Kyle, we were doing laundry that night. No mention of Virginia at all. I started to pull into the driveway, but Kyle wildly shook his hands, gesturing for me to park on the street. I parked and got out of the car. Kyle was so excited that he was talking about one hundred miles an hour. I couldn't understand a word he was saying. He had the remote control in his hand for the garage and pressed a button. The door opened, and inside was a gorgeous brand-new dark-green Porsche. He held his hand up to me as if to say, "Stay right there." He then ran to the car, started it up, and backed it out. He stopped right by me and told me to hop in. I was confused, but I got in anyway. As Kyle sped off, Virginia had a huge, odd smile on her face that made me shiver—kind of like the crazy character in a scary movie. My mind raced. *What was all this about?*

While Kyle was driving, he mentioned that he got off work early and that Virginia came over to spend the day with him. They had been lying in the sun in our yard talking about their dreams and wishes. He happened to mention that his favorite car was a Porsche and one day he would own one. The next words out of her mouth were "Stand up. We are going to the dealership and buying you a brand-new one." He said he could hardly believe his ears, but something made his feet move. To this day, we still laugh about how ridiculous this all was, but in the moment, it was very real to Kyle. I was certainly buying it also.

The plot thickens when you understand that Virginia drove an old banger. Her excuse was that her Mercedes was in the shop and she was driving the car she let her "maids" use. We never questioned it. We were honest people and assumed she was too. Virginia took Kyle that day in her old banger to the Porsche dealership, and still no red flags went up for him. She was rich beyond belief, she adored us, we took her in when it seemed she had no other friends. It seemed crazy but logical. We had never seen the castle she lived in, the pool, the maids, or anything else of it, but Virginia spoke with so much conviction that it was hard not to believe her. And we had no reason to distrust her.

I did make a few comments to Kyle that this could not be for real as he drove us around with a dreamy look in his eyes. He didn't want to hear any of it and just pressed his foot to the pedal. When we got home, Kyle washed every inch of the car and placed a cover over it before he put it to "bed" in the garage. Virginia, Kyle, and I made some food on the grill and watched movies until we all fell asleep on the couches in the living room.

Sometime during the night, I felt the weight of something next to me on the couch. I awoke to Virginia about three inches away from my face. She was saying stupid things that sounded like she was flirting with me. A flood of thoughts came to me, and reality hit me like a slap on the face. Virginia was a lesbian, and everything she had done was for one purpose only, and that was to get to me. I promptly threatened her and pushed her away. She was only about four feet tall, so it was easy to flick her away like a bug. She fell onto the floor, and I told her in no circumstances that I was not interested. I also mentioned that I now knew why she was being so nice to me and Kyle. She bought him the Porsche so that his shiny new toy kept him occupied while she tried to make time with me. I started shouting loudly enough to wake him up. I told him everything that had just occurred. I could not believe my ears when Virginia denied it all. I felt crazy and didn't know where to turn. Kyle trusted me. We were best friends and roommates, but because of the Porsche, he wanted to make sure I just hadn't misunderstood her intentions.

After some time, we finally got Virginia to confess that she was in love with me and had thrown all these things at us in order to be my girlfriend. We asked her to leave and quickly locked the door once she was gone. There was no mention of the car, but Kyle's face fell when he realized that she would be back for the Porsche at some point.

It was already one o'clock in the morning, but we could not stop talking about the situation and chatted for about an hour more. Kyle looked at his watch and mentioned that we had better get to bed since we both had work the next day. I hugged him and off we went to our bedrooms. I was so happy Virginia was out of the house and I fell into my bed, exhausted and fell asleep immediately. I woke up to the doorbell ringing. I opened my eyes and saw that it was still dark outside. Then, I glanced at the clock. What the heck? It was four-thirty in the morning. A feeling washed over me that it was probably Virginia, coming back for the car. I stumbled to the door and met up with Kyle in the hallway, who was also still half asleep. We both mentioned the name "Virginia" as we moved our barking dogs out of the way in order to open the door. Kyle poked his head out and was shocked to see two policemen at the door. He nearly fell over when they asked if he was Kyle so-and-so. When he said yes, they told him he was under arrest. They asked Kyle to step outside. Kyle asked if he could change his clothes first, but they would not allow it. One policeman promptly read out his rights and handcuffed him for the crime of grand theft auto. We were shocked beyond belief and figured this was some sort of retaliation from Virginia. The cops asked me to open the garage door for them. Even though we kept trying to tell them what had happened, they wanted no part of listening. They were on their radios calling in the car and license-plate information. They pushed Kyle's head down and placed him in the back seat of the police car. He was not saying a word but was definitely in panic mode. I told him not to worry and that I would follow along in my car. I ran into the house and promptly grabbed a coat, my purse, and the keys to my car. I was able to follow the police car to the station with the intention of bailing Kyle out of jail.

Everything unfolded at the police station. Apparently, while Virginia was at the desk pretending to purchase the car for Kyle, she had only made arrangements for a sixty-minute test drive. To this day, I cannot believe anyone let them test drive that car without going with them. Unheard of. People in those days were much more trusting (and stupid) than they are today. We found out later that the police had been waiting at Virginia's house all day after the dealership called them. She had spent most of the day and night at our house until we kicked her out. As soon as she arrived home, the police arrested her. She had given them our address and told them that Kyle had the car. That was all the police would tell us except for the fact that Kyle was in big trouble.

Kyle's bail was *way* too high for me to get him out. The charge carried a fine of $100,000 and a penalty of up to five years in a state prison. That meant about 10 percent of that money had to be given to a bail bondsman. I had no choice but to call Kyle's parents. Then the shit really hit the fan. Kyle's parents came and bailed him out. They then asked both of us to come to their house so they could yell and scream at us for hours because we had been so stupid.

We did not make it to work that next day and Kyle had to go see the attorney that his Mom and Dad paid for. I was asked to go as a witness to help explain Kyle's story. The lawyer started out by taking a picture out of a manila folder. He asked us if we recognized the woman in the picture. It was unmistakably Virginia. We told the lawyer every bit of information we could remember about her, including places she took us to eat and shop.

Lucky for us, everyone believed that Kyle was an innocent (and stupid) victim. Virginia was a wanted criminal who had a twenty-year history of crime— everything from credit-card fraud to stealing cars. She was not rich; she was not an attorney. She was a criminal who was the best liar we had ever seen. Even the meal at the steakhouse was paid for with a fraudulent credit card.

We both had to appear in court. Kyle was there with his attorney, and I was there with Kyle's parents as a material witness. It took hardly any time at all. Apparently, Virginia was still in jail and there was so much evidence against her that she would likely stay there for a very long time. The judge dismissed the case against Kyle, but not before he shook his finger at both of us and told us that we needed to smarten up. He never used the word "stupid" but he might as well have.

This was one of the scariest experiences of our lives. I wish I could say that we got smarter at that point, but Virginia was only one in a long list of losers I would encounter.

The Moral: All that glitters is *not* gold.

5 JEFF–THE "CAPTAIN" LOSER

One Friday, Kyle and I both had the day off and decided to show up to a club for its famous crab fest happy hour. It was about six o'clock in the evening, and we were feasting on crab legs and sipping frozen drinks while watching the sun slowly set from our balcony seats. We were dressed casually in shorts, tank tops, and flip-flops. This was a perfect moment: we were taking in life, enjoying that lazy Florida summer night.

Before too long, a shadow was standing before us. We couldn't see detail because we were looking into the bright setting sun, but we could see the outline of a man in a suit and hat. "May I join you?" came out of his mouth, and we quickly looked around and saw that the bar had become so crowded that seats were at a premium. We had an extra chair at our table and welcomed him to sit down. We gave each other "the look" and made a mental note that we really should move the extra chair next time. It had been a hard week, and we didn't feel like socializing. Soon we were shaking hands with Jeff, who was wearing an airline uniform, hat, and name tag. We lived close to Tampa airport and had met up with loads of stewards and stewardesses in our time, but this uniform looked different. We found out that Jeff was an airline pilot. We had never met a pilot in a social setting, and both of us were interested now in speaking to him and hearing all about his adventures. He never took his hat off. He had sweeping blond bangs under the brim of his hat.

Jeff was so knowledgeable. He wowed us with stories of flying, including the gory details of his many cabin crews and parties. He was interesting and seemed so intelligent that we were sucked in as if on tractor beams.

We happened to be hosting a dinner party the next night for some people Kyle worked with. Kyle invited Jeff to the dinner party, and it was perfectly fine with me. I loved the folks Kyle worked with, but I was definitely interested in speaking to Jeff some more. At this point, it never occurred to either of us what Jeff was doing at a gay bar in the first place. We wondered if he had just been driving by in his rented car, taking in the sites of Tampa, and decided to join the large crowd lining up to get inside. We never asked about his sexual preference, and he never told. He was simply an acquaintance we were both enjoying.

Jeff showed up at our home about thirty minutes prior to dinner. He was once again in his airline uniform. Kyle and I thought it was strange because Jeff clearly mentioned that he was off from work for the weekend. Was he trying to impress our dinner guests? Did the airline lose his luggage? It sent up a red flag for us both. We didn't ask because it didn't affect our dinner plans, so who cared in the end? During dinner, Jeff dominated the conversation. As it turned out, when we were in a quiet place and could hear words that were not being drowned out by music, he was quite chatty. Our guests were loving it as he repeated *all* the stories he had shared with Kyle and me the night before. It was like replaying a tape as he recounted word for word. He seemed harmless enough, but no wonder he came into strange bars looking for company. He probably did not have many friends. With his flying schedule and his repeat stories, he surely couldn't get close to people. What was also weird was that he kept his hat on all through dinner. What kind of person goes to a dinner party at a house and never removes his hat? Red flag number two or three popped up in our heads. Our dinner guests started leaving around 11:00 p.m. Jeff made no move to go. Although we didn't have to work in the morning, we were both tired, so I just told him it was late and would he mind leaving. He then claimed to have drunk so much alcohol that he didn't feel good about driving back to his hotel. Kyle and I separately poured a lot of drinks that night, so I wasn't keeping track of how much he drank, but he seemed perfectly sober. He asked if he could spend the night.

Kyle and I were aggravated, but we couldn't put someone who claimed he felt drunk out into the night after pouring his drinks, so we agreed to let "Captain Jeff" stay on our couch. He went out to his rental car and brought in a small airline bag. He then proceeded to go into one of the bathrooms and get ready for bed. He came out into our living room looking like a completely different person. He had on a white T-shirt, tighty-whitey underwear, and bare feet. He was really out of shape for an airline pilot. His stomach was sticking way out, which led us to believe that he had been wearing some kind of girdle under that uniform. The craziest thing was that he had no hair on his head anywhere but the front of his head. His beloved pilot's hat was finally off, and he looked like some kind of circus freak. He also looked very old. He was definitely at least twenty or thirty years older than we were. He had a tan on his face, neck and arms only, and I guess that was what made him look younger. His two little legs were skinny and white. He definitely was not spending his downtime at the beach, getting a tan in the tropics.

It's funny how you see someone at sunset or over the glitter of candles at a dinner party and they look wonderful, yet you see them without their uniform and in their underwear and they look like a bum. Perhaps it was because we were tired or slightly annoyed with his performance at dinner, but the transformation was shocking and we were disgusted.

I locked my door that night because there was something eating at my gut about Jeff. I just didn't want to deal with him. Kyle later told me he did the same. Looking back, Jeff could have been an axe murderer for all we knew, and here he was staying in our house. I didn't have to worry, because the dogs always slept with me, but I did go to sleep hoping Kyle would be okay.

When I got up the next morning, Kyle was puttering around in the kitchen and Jeff was sitting at the counter on a bar stool. Kyle, being a gracious host had already served Jeff coffee and he was eating the spread of food that Kyle had put out for him. After about thirty minutes, Jeff excused himself and went into our bathroom to freshen up. He emerged with his uniform and hat on and probably the girdle, because he was looking thinner and dapper again. We could not take our eyes off him, because his appearance had changed so much. It was like someone putting on a Halloween costume.

He told us that he would visit some relative on the east coast of Florida that day before heading back to the airport and home to Chicago the next day. But before he left, he handed both Kyle and me a business card. The card had his airline logo and a phone number to reach him. He explained that he would love to have us on one of his flights sometime and to give him a call if we ever wanted to fly for free. Kyle and I were so excited. It had all been worth it. So he was a bit annoying, who cared? So he was really ugly under his magic uniform and girdle. Who cared? We could fly anywhere in the world for *free*, and he also offered us a pilot's free hotel stay. Jeff left, and Kyle and I began to argue about where we would use our golden ticket. Should we fly to Australia? Germany? Where would we go?

About three weeks later, Kyle and I decided that we would like to fly to Europe. The plan was to get to France and then spend some time taking the railway around Europe. We had no idea how to make reservations for our flights or our hotels, so we settled in with some wine to call Jeff.

We thought we were so cool putting our telephone on speaker as we sat there sipping wine, ready to plan the most fabulous vacation ever. Jeff picked up the phone and assured us that he would make all the reservations for us. We settled on a date about two months away, and Jeff told us he would call us back with all the details.

The next week, true to his word, he phoned us back with details. We spent the next few weeks giving those details to our bosses and making plans. We were all set to meet him at Tampa airport at the ticket reservation desk for his airline. Kyle and I had shopped till we dropped, packed all of our new clothes in suitcases, and Kyle's mom would be dropping us off at the airport. We had good friends coming to take care of the dogs each day, and we were on our way. We had told everyone we knew about our good fortune and taken time off work for this vacation. Everyone was completely jealous, and that made the trip even better.

We went to the airport so excited that we did nothing but talk and interrupt each other's words in the car. Kyle's Mom kept yelling at us to keep it down. Finally she pulled up to the airport and we each kissed her goodbye. She popped the trunk and we went to collect our suitcases out of it. Then we walked inside, our suitcases wheeling behind us. We were still talking the entire time. We arrived at the ticket desk and Jeff wasn't there yet. We waited and waited and waited, but Jeff never showed up. Of course we thought it was some kind of mistake. We had the wrong date, he had the wrong date. So many "what ifs" were running through our heads. We went to a pay phone to make a call to Jeff's number. The number had been disconnected. We nearly fell over. This happened literally overnight because we had spoken to Jeff on this number the day before.

After about six hours, we realized that Jeff was not coming. We went to the airline desk and asked about him. The agent looked him up and found that nobody by his name worked at the company. He also pointed out that the business cards we had for Jeff were fake. The man at the desk showed us his business card, which looked nothing like the ones we had.

We quickly went back to the pay phone and called Kyle's mom to come and pick us up. She made comments through the phone about how she would die an early death with all the stress we were causing her. That never did happen, and she is still alive and well at ninety-plus years old.

We walked out of the airport like two little dogs with our tails between our legs. Kyle's mom yelled at us all the way home and dropped us off at our driveway. Kyle dug through his backpack for our front-door keys, and we both stepped in. The dogs knocked both of us over and we dropped our bags to give them attention and greet them. They were so excited to see us that it almost made everything OK again. Normally, it did not take long for them to settle down, but today they seemed antsy, and we couldn't figure out why. We guessed they had been so upset by seeing us leave with suitcases, that they were now thrilled for us to be home. We decided that before we went to unpack, we would put their leashes on and take them for a quick walk to the park. We were in no hurry to start the unpleasant task of unpacking. There was no rush. We left the suitcases in the hall and went out to enjoy the walk.

Once we got home, the dogs plodded into the kitchen for water and we carried our bags into our rooms. It was then that I heard Kyle screaming. Me and the dogs ran to his room to see what had happened. Kyle was standing in the middle of his room frantically screaming "we were robbed". Every piece of anything good in his room was gone. Kyle was the male version of a fashionista, and his taste was exquisite. He wouldn't wear or use anything cheap if his life depended on it. All his clothing, shoes, and jewelry were designer-label stuff. Kyle was missing three-quarters of his room. His cologne, suits, shoes— everything was gone except for what he had purchased and packed for the trip. For me, it was just a few pieces of jewelry that were not really important. I was wearing all my good stuff for the trip. Of course it hit both of us at that very moment that Jeff had somehow done this or was involved with someone that had. No wonder the dogs had been acting so weird. The dogs also knew Jeff, because he had stayed overnight with us and each time our circle of friends grew, the dogs just accepted them as part of us. Still, the dogs had seen something out of the ordinary today, and it had upset them. If only they could talk, we thought.

We called the police, and they took about forty-five minutes to arrive. We told them all about Jeff and our fake trip and that we suspected he was the one to rob our house that day while we waited for him at the airport. We could not believe this was happening to us. The police assured us that things like this were everyday occurrences and that we had to stop trusting people so much. Since Jeff had been at our house for dinner, his fingerprints were all over the place. The police ran them through but got no hits on the Florida criminal databases. The police assured us that Jeff must have stolen that uniform and hat and made up his own business cards. No wonder we had never seen him before at any of our hangouts. He disappeared from our lives as fast as he had appeared in them.

The Moral: You may look at someone in a uniform as someone in a position of authority. Listen to that little voice in your head. If there are red flags, you should pay attention. There are no free rides on an airline or anywhere else in life.

6 DOMINIC–THE PERVERT BUG-KILLING LOSER

This loser is so awful that I nearly left him out of this book. I did not wish to relive these memories at all. I thought about it a long time and decided that the story was one of the most important and that if it would help even one person, then it needed to be told.

Kyle and I had both been complaining for what seemed like forever about our jobs. If you could speak to our families, then you would understand that collectively we had more jobs than any other people we knew. We had tried them all. Restaurant server, host/hostess, retail managers, skin-care specialists, German dancer, receptionist, and so many others that I could write a book about the jobs alone.

One day, we took our local newspaper outside to our picnic table with some wine spritzers and the intention of finding yet another line of work for us both. We wanted something totally new and wanted to work together if possible. Kyle and I had each other's backs. We could trust each other and thought we would be the perfect instant team for anyone's business.

The ad was a little crazy. It had a picture of a huge palmetto bug (like a big crunchy roach). Normally, I would not be inclined to read further, but that bug was so huge that we just had to know what it was all about. It contained words such as "free training," "unlimited income," "no experience necessary," and "be your own boss." Kyle and I were shouting the words out and getting more excited by the minute. The only prerequisites were that you needed to look and conduct yourself in a professional manner with clients. Nobody has had more experience dealing with people than we did. We knew we were both hardworking and had received many accolades in our jobs.

As we read on, it turned out that the company needed salespeople to visit various corporations and sell them monthly pest-control contracts. Anyone who has ever lived in Florida knows that without monthly pest control, every ounce of food and living/working space would be overrun with palmetto bugs. It was a consistent business, and we figured we would never be out of work. For some reason, there was no phone number to call. There was an address only, and everyone had to apply in person. We thought this was great and would save time to meet the employer and apply all in one day. Our resumes were in tip-top shape, so we needed to focus on our clothes.

We were on our way to a new life. We clinked our glasses together and decided that we'd better get into the house and find our best outfits.

We needed to look more professional than ever before, since the ad specifically stated this. Kyle always had an array of suits already put together, so we would start with my outfit. We headed into my bedroom with the dogs naturally following along. Kyle sat on my bed with his glass of wine, and I proceeded to pull out hangers one by one so he could help me choose. He said, "The purple dress with that cream suit jacket would be stunning. And you could wear your cream sandals to match the ensemble." I rifled through the heap of shoes on my closet floor and finally found the second cream sandal. I laid it all out on the chair in my room to look at it. Of course all three dogs had to go and sniff and lick at it, so I had to get a wet washcloth and wipe off the dog snot. I moved the outfit back into the closet for the next morning so it wouldn't get any more dog slime. Kyle helped me choose toned-down, business-like jewelry to go with it. That was it. I was ready.

We then moved to Kyle's room and switched roles. I plopped onto his king-sized, perfectly made bed and quickly put my wine on the table while I waited for all three dogs to get comfortable on the bed before I drank it. Otherwise, there would be a spill disaster. Kyle allowed only white wine in his room for this reason. After a few seconds, I leaned up on the pillows, my legs and feet surrounded by dogs, and waited for Kyle to go through his closet. He brought out so many beautiful suits, and we chose a gray one. A crisp white shirt with gray stripes and a black-and-gray tie would pull together the entire look. Kyle was fussier than I was. All his shoes were polished, wrapped in tissue, and carefully put away in individual boxes. They were also clearly marked on the outside with descriptions. It didn't take him long to bring out the perfect black shoes.

Our clothes were ready, but we decided we needed to go all out for this. At the time, Kyle worked for a skin-care company and got on the phone to make appointments for facials. He also wanted to stop by his barber and get a trim. We could walk to the plaza where both of these businesses were. We put on some flip-flops and walked and chatted in the beautiful Florida sunshine. We were uplifted and excited about the next morning. We both had to be at work the next day, but not until later. We intended to interview, go home to change, and report to our jobs immediately afterward. We were also hoping to give our two weeks' notice if we got the new jobs.

We got our facials and felt wonderful. We were in bed by nine o'clock that night in order to look our best. When we got up at five o'clock, we felt wonderful and refreshed, ready for interviews. We took our showers and primped ourselves to a flawless finish. On our way out to the garage, we stopped and admired ourselves in the mirrored hallway. Damn, we looked good. There was no way they were turning us down.

Back in the days before GPS, finding addresses was a struggle. Kyle would drive, and I would navigate. This place had an address on a busy main road, and we drove past it five times before we finally found it. The sun-soaked numbers on the unmarked door were barely visible. It looked like a shit hole. We had pictured a huge office with white marble and windows. We justified the condition of the office by remembering that our jobs would take us on the road. It did not matter what the office looked like because we would never be in it.

We finally found a place to park, several blocks away, and headed to the door.

It looked like a scene from a *Godfather* movie. There were clumps of Italian-looking men sitting around eating pasta and sandwiches. There was a pool table in the back and people playing on it. None of them were dressed up. They all had casual pants and golf shirts or shirts with rolled-up sleeves and no ties. The place was grungy and smelled like alcohol. We thought we walked into a bar instead of a place of employment. A large, fat guy was on the phone and motioned for Kyle and me to sit in the chairs in front of his desk.

When he hung up, he reached his hand over the desk in order to shake my hand first. He said, "My name is Dominic. What can I do for yas?" I, introduced myself and Kyle and explained that we were there for the sales jobs. He flashed a huge smile and said, "Oh good, good," and he spun around to a table behind him with lots of papers and folders. He grabbed two papers and told us we needed to fill out applications. Kyle said, "We have resumes. Do we still need to fill out applications?" Dominic said, "Oh, yous are very fancy. Sorry, you still gotta fill them out." He was smoking a huge cigar, and it stunk. We got our pens out. I have always thought that the application process was stupid. Some state laws required applications on file for everyone, regardless of resumes.

Once we filled out the applications, Dominic asked us if we wanted any coffee or water. Both of us declined. He took the resumes and applications and started reading through them. He was making comments and noises as if he was impressed. He then explained that he was the owner of the company and he would be our boss. He also explained that the business had lots of technicians but no salespeople. We were the first to be hired. It was a new business, and it would take a while to get going. This explained a lot. We assumed that the place was disheveled but would be getting into shape soon.

He began asking us questions. They were not the normal types of interview questions. They were all personal, about our lives and families and friends. He had a keen interest in mine and Kyle's relationship. Red flags went up all over the place, but we really wanted these jobs. We figured that these goons definitely needed professional faces to sell their products. These were probably the guys who did the pest control and were not used to selling anything to people. Still, they would be the ones going to people's homes. I could not imagine having any of them in my home. But, I supposed that when they had their equipment and uniforms on, they probably looked professional. I stopped thinking about because it sounded like Dominic was wrapping up whatever he had been saying and I needed to pay attention.

Dominic asked us if we had any questions. We asked about money, benefits, and hours. He explained that we could work anytime we wanted and could just drop off our papers in the office once a week to show that we had been visiting customers. We had benefits and would get paid every other week. He told us that the pay was based on commission but the money was "real good" and we would be "rolling in dough" once our customer base grew.

After he answered all our questions, he simply said, "OK, yous will do. You start tomorrow." We both started talking at the same time, explaining that we needed to give notice at our jobs before we could start. He waved his hand in the air and said, "Whoa, whoa, whoa. OK, then you start in two weeks." There were no business cards, no papers, nothing. He just told us to report back to this location in two weeks. He said we would start our training once we arrived and get our bug kits. As we left, Kyle muttered to me sarcastically under his breath, "Oh bug kits—cannot wait for that." I said nothing and kept walking.

When we left, our guts were trying to talk to us. They were sending signals for us to never return. But on the way home we talked about how we would never be in that office with any of them and we could just come and go as we pleased. Also, we discussed the "rolling in dough" part. We couldn't be happier about this. If we had to see those guys once a week, just to turn in our commission invoices, then so be it. After all, we had each other. Nothing bad could happen.

We went back to work that afternoon and gave our notices. Both of us wondered if we were doing the right thing. We were not excited about our new jobs no matter how we tried to talk ourselves into them. Still, we hated our old jobs even more. And, it was a new adventure. We thought if we didn't like the new jobs, we could always quit and start again. So what difference did it make? We also liked the idea of the "make your own hours." We pictured ourselves riding around in Kyle's mustang all day, going where we wanted, when we wanted, and these thoughts were the ones that kept us going. We chose to ignore the little twinges in our guts.

Two weeks went by fast. On the Sunday night before starting work, we were once again going through our ritual of finding just the right outfits. We were ready. We were turning the page and starting our new lives. The next day, we showed up at the pest control company, and Dominic was at the front desk. The place was less crowded—just him and two other guys who seemed busy on the phone. It looked like someone had swept out the office, and it smelled a little fresher.

Dominic led us to a table with two large books on it. They were three-ring binders filled with hundreds of plastic sheets with pictures of big palmetto bugs. He told us to sit down and handed us each a pad and a pen. The pens had big bugs on them too. Even though they were hideous, it was the first professionally branded thing we had seen since we first encountered Dominic and his office.

He explained that we had two days to study the bug materials and would then be knowledgeable enough to go speak to customers about the company's services. He also told us that we would get paid in cash these first two days. We asked if we were going to be tested on the materials. He said, "No way. Yous will be sent out with a bug guy the first few weeks until you know all the right stuff to say." We felt better instantly. Our biggest fear had been put to rest: they didn't expect us to know about extermination after only two days of study.

Dominic told us to help ourselves to anything in the little kitchen. Kyle went in to make us some coffee. He made a joke to me quietly that even though the place was a shit hole, there was probably no bugs in the kitchen. We both laughed out loud over that. Once Kyle got back with the coffee, we devised a plan to read independently in our books, and then stop at the end of every section to quiz each other.

The materials were so boring that we were both falling asleep. Except for the diagrams that had pictures of bugs and their characteristics, they just droned on and on about chemicals used to kill each type of bug and the schedules they required in order to keep them from breeding. Despite the boring subject, we noticed that so far, nobody was watching over our shoulders. This could be the best job we've ever had. We were already enjoying our independence, and things were looking up.

On the second day, Dominic told us we would be visiting our first customers the next morning. He had a list of businesses that he wanted us to go through so we could see the areas of town we would need to cover. We took the list and started toward the door. He said, "Hey, wait a minute," and reached into his pocket. He retrieved a wad of bills so large that his fat sausage fingers had trouble holding them. He gave a handful of hundred-dollar bills to each of us and thanked us for taking the time to train. We looked at each other, took the money, and left. We didn't say one word until we got into the car. Then we both started screaming. We had never made that much money for two days' work. This was beginning to look like a great job.

But, after those initial two days, things got bad. Real bad.

We showed up on day three, and Dominic intended to split us up. Some guy named Paulie was there. Dom told Kyle that he would be going out on the road with Paulie and that I would be going with him. I felt my heart race. I did not want to be separated from Kyle. I said, "Why do Kyle and I have to split up?" He said, "Why? Are you afraid to go out with me?" My mind started racing. Yes I was totally afraid to go out with him alone. I didn't know him, and I didn't know many of the areas where we were going. I would be out with a stranger, boss or not, and headed to the unknown. I was petrified. Still, I heard my voice answer, "No, I just thought Kyle and I would be working together all the time." He pointed out that Kyle and I could cover more territory if we were apart. This was disappointing. We would each need to take our cars every day, and the fun we were planning to have together was not going to happen. I was upset inside. Kyle later told me that he had the exact same reaction but didn't want to complain.

I thought about it as we all left the building and figured that what they didn't know wouldn't hurt them. Once we were on our own, Kyle and I could still work together and cover double the places. I felt a bit better with those thoughts in mind. I made a mental note to discuss with Kyle later.

Dom got out in front and told us to turn right outside the door. He told us they had a private lot in the back where he and the other owners parked. The lot was enclosed in barbed wire. Dominic motioned for me to get into his big car. He said some words like "That's my caddy." I didn't know a great deal about cars, but I knew the word Cadillac and that it was synonymous with expensive. I guess I was supposed to be impressed. It was baby blue and had leather seats and every kind of extra on it that money could buy. I thought Dom looked odd driving it. He was never dressed up, he did not look polished, and his speech was horrible. He just didn't fit the picture of this car. Kyle got into a similar green vehicle, and the cars went off in different directions.

Dominic had music playing in the car and was acting weird—like we were on a date or something. He kept asking me if the car was too cold or if the music was good or too loud. My inner voice was screaming. It was afraid. I was afraid. I had a horrible feeling and could not put my finger on the exact reasons.

A long bridge in Tampa connects the city to St. Petersburg over water. The territories I had seen on the map did not include anything across this bridge. When Dominic started going over the bridge, I asked him what we were doing. I mentioned that none of the customers from our sales territory sheets were on the other side of the bridge. He told me to relax and that he had to stop home for a few minutes. We would be heading back immediately afterward. I started thinking about the contents of my purse and what I might have to use as a weapon if I needed it. I also hoped he lived in a neighborhood with lots of people so I could jump out and run to another house. I was preparing myself mentally for something bad.

He must have noticed that I was stressed out. He mentioned that his wife, "Candy," was home and was looking forward to meeting me. All my tension disappeared. I was being silly. I had to stop watching scary movies and violent television shows. My imagination had run wild. I had misjudged poor Dominic. He was just being gracious and friendly in the car.

We pulled up to his house. It was quite lovely. Definitely a high end setting. He had neighbors, but they were not right on top of one another. There was plenty of room in between. When we drove up the driveway, I could see a pool area that was totally gorgeous. It had a large kidney-shaped pool, a pool house, chairs, a grill, and a shaded porch with tables and chairs. There was also a beautiful area with chairs for sunbathing. It was surrounded with colorful flowers. It looked like paradise. I mentioned this to Dominic, and he proudly told me that Candy had done it all. He was bragging about her, and I was feeling better and better.

He opened the front door for me. The hallway was long and had cathedral ceilings. It was light and airy. There were several doors on either side of the hallway with a kitchen at the end. He pointed to the kitchen as if to tell me this was the way we were headed.

The kitchen was enormous. There were counters everywhere as well as a huge island in the middle with lovely white leather chairs. It was one of the most beautiful houses I had been in. He called out to his wife, "Candy, we are here." We waited a bit, and Candy wasn't coming out. Dominic asked me if I wanted something to drink. He brought out a crystal liquor vase full of what looked like whiskey. I declined and told him I didn't drink hard liquor. I thanked him just the same. He said, "Suit yourself" and poured himself a water glass full of the stuff. I was worried because he had to drive us back to the office. I said nothing. He excused himself and said he was going to find Candy. He disappeared down the hallway.

I sat in one of the white leather chairs to wait. It swallowed me up with comfort. I enjoyed looking around while I was waiting. It is always fun to see how others decorate, including colors they use. Soon, I heard footsteps coming from the hallway. Nothing could have prepared me for the shock I was about to have. Candy was walking into the kitchen stark naked. She was about twenty years older than I was. She had short blond hair, and her skin was tanned everywhere. She was not pretty, she was not ugly, but to this day I remember every bit of her very clearly. She came into the kitchen and said, "Hi, I am Candy." Dominic was behind her, watching my face.

I couldn't control myself and started to cry. I shrieked and said, "What is happening here? Why am I here? I don't want any of this." Dominic started screaming at me and said, "You little bitch, I own you. You will do whatever I say you will do. Nobody knows you are here, and you aren't going anywhere." Candy was clearly uncomfortable. She said, "Dom, are you crazy? She is about the same age as your own daughter. What can you be thinking? You told me she was older."

I then ran up and hugged her. I said, "Please, Candy, I am just like your daughter. I am innocent, and I don't know anything about this kind of thing and don't want to. Please don't make me do this. Please don't let him hurt me or touch me." I was shaking and crying so hard that she just petted my hair and said, "Don't worry, hun, nothing is going to happen to you." I realized that Dominic was nowhere in sight.

When he returned, he was still swearing and shouting and shaking his fist at me. A miracle happened. Candy told him, "Bring her back, Dom. Bring her back right now."

He was so pissed off and turned and walked swiftly down the hall to open the front door. He slammed it behind him so hard that I could feel the hallway floor shake. Candy squeezed my hand and whispered to me, "Let him take you back to work. Don't refuse the ride. His bark is worse than his bite, and he may be mad, but it will be okay. But, if you run away it won't go well." I nodded my head and squeezed her hand. I asked if she would be OK, and she winked at me. I had no idea at this point if Dominic had forced her into this and she would suffer when he got home. I left her side and walked down the hallway with jelly legs and a sick stomach. When I opened the front door, Dominic was in the car sitting behind the steering wheel. The car was started, and I was afraid to get in. But I remembered what Candy had said. I did not refuse the ride.

Once I was in the car with the door closed, Dom started shouting and screaming: "You cunt, if I get home and find out you insulted my Candy, this will be the last day you live. And you'd better not tell nobody what happened here today either. No way is some little bitch going to ruin my life." I was crying my eyes out and screamed back. "She was *not* insulted. She was understanding, and she was nice. When you get home later, you will find that out." I also told him that I would be embarrassed to tell anyone what had happened—that I was ashamed at how stupid I had been. He said, "You'd better be right about that." He berated me all the way back to the office, but I did not care as long as we were heading toward the bridge to Tampa and to that office.

When we got to the barbed-wire lot, I jumped out of the car and started to run. I didn't know where I was going. I just ran. Dom did not try to stop me or speak to me. To this day, I feel lucky and it scares me to think of the "what if's".

There was a restaurant a couple of doors away. I ran into it because it felt safe to be with people. I asked if the restaurant had a phone I could use, and someone pointed me to a pay phone. I couldn't call Kyle. I had no idea where he was. I was worried. Had he encountered a similar situation? Were these people involved in some sex ring or human trafficking or something?

I couldn't call the police. Kyle might die as a result, and after Dominic's ranting, I believed what he said. At that moment, I decided I would never tell anyone about this except for Kyle.

The only thing I could think to do was to get a taxi home. At least if I was home, Kyle could reach me by telephone if he needed to. If one of us were home, we could watch out for the other one. I called a taxi company, and within twenty minutes I was on my way home. In the taxi, I was trying to send Kyle mental vibes that I was home. Thinking about this now, having a mobile phone would have been great.

After another twenty minutes, I saw my hand shaking as I put my key into the lock. All at once, I was being greeted by my dogs. I cried when I saw them and shut the door behind me. I hugged them, so grateful to be home and safe with them. I just sank to the floor, and they surrounded me. Thank heaven for the dogs. They seemed to sense that I was upset and were trying their best to comfort me. If for any reason Dominic planned on coming to my house or sending someone else there, my three Dobermans would be happy to greet them. Nobody would ever hurt me here.

Within ten minutes, the phone was ringing. It was Kyle. "Why are you home? How did you get there?" I didn't answer either question and instead asked him if he was OK. He sounded puzzled and said, "Yes, why wouldn't I be?" I said, "Kyle, do not say a word on your end. Just listen." I told him that he had to make any excuse possible to leave that office now. I asked him if Dominic was there, and he said, "Yes." I felt sick and shaky again. I said, "Kyle, I mean it. Leave now."

It seemed like hours had passed before I heard Kyle's Mustang drive up. I had showered with the hottest water I could take. Although nobody touched me that day, I felt dirty and could not shake the feeling. When Kyle came into the front door, I hugged him so tightly that I nearly suffocated him. He mentioned that he had gotten back to the office and saw Dominic on the phone, but not me and was puzzled. He figured that we finished early and assumed Dom had given me a ride home, and that prompted his call to me. He could see that I was visibly shaken and had been crying.

He asked me what was wrong. We went into the living room, and I told him everything. He was also scared. He kept talking about how he had been in the office with them after this had happened. He was also going through "what if's". We wanted to call the police because we didn't know what any of them were capable of and we didn't want Dominic to do this to another person. Plus, we had no idea if Candy would be in any kind of jeopardy. In the moment, we just couldn't do it. We were too scared. We were in fear for our lives.

Whether it was good or bad, Kyle and I decided not to breathe a word of what happened to anyone. And just to be safe, we moved (again). We broke our lease and didn't care if we lost our security deposit. We could not stay knowing that these criminals knew where we lived. We had a friend, Peter, who lived in a house with a huge fenced-in yard. He was the type of person who would let us invite ourselves over with no questions asked. We took the dogs and stayed all night.

The next morning, we felt safe and things looked brighter. Although we vowed never to talk about the situation, we did share with Peter what had happened. He hadn't bugged us for an explanation, but we felt we owed it to him. It turned out to be a good thing because as luck would have it, Peter had just lost two roommates and asked if we wanted to move in. We hadn't spent much of the cash that Dominic had handed us, so we handed it over to Peter and paid our rent up for the month. Peter had always been one of our best friends and we had known him for years. We had worked together, we knew each other's families and he would not be the typical roommate we had learned to dread.

That afternoon, we spent time looking through the want ads. We both needed jobs. We would never again apply to some small unknown company. We applied for work at a huge hotel with thousands of tourists around all day, every day. We got those jobs and turned the page once again.

The Moral: No matter how old you are, never, ever go anywhere with a stranger, even if they are your boss. People can use their position of power to intimidate you, but when you feel that happening and something doesn't seem right, it's not. Don't be afraid to say no.

7 LES–THE "RUNAWAY" LOSER

Because of Les, this book has taken me two extra years to finish. He is partially responsible for its creation, but this loser broke my heart and put my life into a tailspin like no other. This loser's story is the saddest in the book, but perhaps it will help others put their lives back together again. Les was also one of two losers in this book (see Dina, the "old sock") who saved me the trouble of cutting them out because he did it first.

I met Les through a mutual friend, Dan, whom I worked with. These two friends had been involved in crime at one point in their lives. Both boys took a bad path and met while incarcerated shortly for some teenage pranks. The crimes were not against humanity, but instead disorderly, drunken nights out when they disturbed the peace of Tampa, Florida. This did not derail me from keeping Dan as a friend, nor did it sway me away from a relationship with Les. Perhaps I ignored pertinent information that would later shape who Les was, but I will never know.

What can I tell you? Les was an amazing, charismatic person who could put his hand to anything. He worked for the city of Tampa high up in a cherry-picking machine, cutting branches away from power lines. He was active and in great shape and was up for any adventure at any time. He was tall and had dark-blond hair, green eyes, and a noble face and jawline. Kyle had also met him and got along well with him. It is always a plus when your best friend likes your new boyfriend.

I worked in a high-end, gorgeous hotel/restaurant at the time and attended some classes during the day. If you know the service industry, you know that you work nights, holidays, and weekends. The upside is that all of your coworkers do too, and this brings a special closeness with them. Les fit in with all the folks I worked with like a glove. Whenever he could be with us, he was there. We had days and nights at the beach, where we played volleyball and other games and had campfires and conversation. We all got to know Les well, and I was comfortable dating him after a while.

We had a whirlwind romance. He made me feel good about myself all the time, and I gained a feeling of security whenever I was with him. He was six-foot-four, and at five-foot-ten, I could wear high heels whenever I pleased and not be taller than my partner. After a year, with no fanfare whatsoever, Les one day said, "I want this happiness always. Will you marry me?" I said yes, and our plan to start a life together began. We were both twenty-four years old, so we had a lifetime of happiness to look forward to. My family lived in New York and had never met Les. His parents lived in Tampa, and I had never met either of them. We decided that we should start making plans to get married. We didn't set a date for the wedding because we wanted to speak to everyone first and have the family involved in the fun of planning it. We were never in a hurry and just worked hard and enjoyed the time together and with our friends.

The first family meeting took place at Les' parents' house. These people were at least twenty-five years older than my parents, and somehow I hadn't expected that. Les seemed so energetic and on the go all the time that I couldn't imagine these older, weak people chasing after him. They were definitely not the type to want to go places and do things with us. In fact, his dad, Stan, who was eighty-five, was mentally sharp as a tack but physically did not fare so well. His mother, Pam, was in her late sixties and was physically not sick but was stranger than strange. When I walked into their home the first time, she could not get up to greet me because she was having coffee with her pet squirrel, Shirley the Squirrely, who would sit on her shoulder. The squirrel was a baby, and she had rescued it from a cat in her yard. Shirley hated everyone but Pam and would hiss and claw if people got too close. I didn't get a chance to shake her hand, hug her, or anything of that nature. The table and red pleather rounded booth had been purchased from a local restaurant that was going out of business. Pam gestured for me to sit and join them, but Les and his dad were crammed at one end. I pushed Les aside to sit near him in order to get as far away from Shirley as possible. I was afraid, and her side of the booth was surrounded by squirrel shit. They offered coffee or tea, but I could not stomach the thought of eating anything from this table.

The conversation was normal, but Pam had complete control of everything Les' dad said and did. He was the supreme doormat and couldn't take a shit without her saying it was OK. She also had a nasty habit of clicking her dentures in and out of her mouth. The clicking from her and Shirley every few seconds was annoying. To top this off, a cuckoo clock above her on the wall was broken and cuckooed more than the usual increments. The house was dismal and had thick, dark curtains. Most people who live in Florida prefer to take advantage of a light, sunny house since they have that option 365 days a year. Pam, however, preferred this vampire-like setting, but I wondered if the squirrel shit was the only filth I was sitting in. This atmosphere was hard to understand because Les and Dan had a spotless apartment. I wondered how this divide happened and how Les turned into such a neat freak.

We went to their house at least once a week after that, and I learned a lot about Les and his family. I had known that Les and his siblings were adopted because Les' dad could not have children, but I also heard for the first time, all the stories of each adoption. These people were strange, but good hearted and despite my first negative thoughts, I admired them for taking in these children that needed homes. I learned that all his siblings lived close by. On the scale of age ranges, his sister Vivvy was about fifty-eight, their sister Lydia was about thirty, and the baby was Les, who was twenty-four. Pam told me that they had met Les' mom when Vivvy worked at a home for unwed mothers. Apparently she was from Sweden and had gotten into trouble, had the baby, let Pam and Stan adopt him, and then moved back to Sweden with her family. They were thrilled to get Les, the only boy, and he quickly became the apple of their eyes. Vivvy was nice enough, but she was so much older that I never really had anything in common with her. She was also the closest to Pam, so they were usually together chatting, and it made me feel like somewhat of an outsider.

Les' sister Lydia was wonderful. She was married to a Cuban man named Carlos, and they had three children together. When we went to their house for barbecues, it was always fun. They were closer to our age and therefore more relatable. The oddity was that Pam didn't get along well with Lydia. Even though she had raised her, she was overbearing and insulted her. Lydia couldn't do anything right in her eyes, and Pam criticized her in front of everyone. Pam seemed to take issue with the fact that Lydia was so close to Carlos's family. Although I saw the strain, I never got my nose into it. Everyone treated me well, and I didn't want to get involved in anything negative.

Next it was time to take Les and his parents to New York to meet my family. My brother was living in Canada while attending medical school, so he was not home to meet them. My parents were the exact opposite in every way to Les' parents. They were younger, still working, healthy, and eager to do things and go places with us. When Les' mother arrived at their home, her attitude notably changed. I could not put my finger on it, but she became quiet. I took her up to the room where they would be staying to show her around. While we were up there, I asked her flat out if something was wrong. She mumbled something about "rich people" and basically told me that she didn't feel comfortable. My parents were far from rich, but their house was clean and cared for. I guess that was the difference. I thought the whole thing was strange because everyone always loved going to my parents' home and found them to be open, welcoming, and down to earth. Their home was beautiful, but it was because they worked hard all of their lives and never had a thing handed to them. They also had pride in their home and were always painting, cleaning and keeping it up. I resented her attitude and snapped at her with some retort I don't recall. I was sick in my stomach as we headed back into the living room.

When we got there, a spread with drinks and food was waiting for us. My mother was always a wonderful hostess and treated all who came like royalty. Pam sat next to Stan, and I sat next to Les. When Stan tried to reach for food and drinks, Pam shouted out and told him not to eat a thing. She told him that his health was poor enough and she would not be the one having a bad time if he ate the wrong thing. Instead, she pulled sandwiches out of her bag that she had prepared and brought with her from Florida. They asked my mother for water, and she and Stan ate the sandwiches instead of my mother's food. Les looked sick, and I could tell he wanted to crawl away somewhere. My parents were gracious. After Les' parents had gone to bed, my parents assured us that their quirky behavior was not a problem. They did not want Les to feel bad, and they didn't want anyone to feel uncomfortable in their home.

The rest of the visit was hard, especially for my parents. They should be inducted into the good books as saints after the treatment they received the next few days. I kept talking to them and apologizing for Pam's behavior, but they told me not to worry. They laughed and said Pam was old and set in her ways and that we should all just "let it go". Les and I were staying another week after his parents went back, and I knew our time would be fun once they were gone. But the time with them was agonizing.

Once my Dad dropped off Les' parents at the airport, we had a fabulous week.

Everyone got along and got to know one another. Les and my dad had so much in common. My dad showed Les all the work he had done in the backyard with his patio stones and garden. He also bragged about me, and told Les the story of how I had helped him build and paint the fence years before that. He told Les that I had worked as hard as some of the men he normally worked with on his construction jobs. It made me feel really proud. My mother did mention to me in private that Les was nothing like his parents. When I reminded her he had been adopted, she said "oh yes, well no wonder," and we both laughed.

Before we left to go back to Florida, my mother nailed down a venue for our wedding, which would take place in October of that year, on my birthday. The wedding was only about ten months away and would be a beautiful event with only family, still bringing the attendance up to around one hundred. I remember the nagging feeling in my stomach as we spoke about it. My mother was making all these fabulous plans, and I wondered how Les' mother would take the news that they would have to come back to New York for the wedding. Les assured me that she had a choice. She could come or choose not to. He told me to stop worrying.

Those months flew by, and soon we were back in New York for our wedding. Pam and Stan would be flying in a few days later. None of Les' family was planning to attend except for his parents. Vivvy was in poor health, and Lydia was up to her ass in alligators with family, work and school. In addition, she was about 8 months pregnant with their third child and in those days, the airlines did not allow you to fly in that condition. She also knew the drive would be horrendous for her. They all wished us well, and we promised to share pictures and experiences as soon as we were home in Tampa again.

The wedding was amazing, and so many great memories were made that evening. Stan and Pam basically sat in one place all night and the family lined up to meet them one by one, as if they were royalty. My family is absolutely accommodating and amazing and Les' parents were treated like gold. Stan was gracious but not allowed to say much, and Pam talked endlessly about Shirley the Squirrely. My family did not care. Being in a large family you have your share of everything and everyone was very accepting and happy for us.

Les and I had one honeymoon night at the Hilton, and my always accommodating parents took Stan and Pam home with them. The next afternoon, my dad drove them to the airport. As crazy as this may sound, I immediately knew that I got pregnant that night with my first child. I felt it; I knew it, and nobody could tell me anything different. We were off to a wonderful life together.

I quit my job at the restaurant because it is difficult to share a life with someone when your hours are exact opposite. I had finished school and was gainfully employed at an upscale real estate company before I met Les. Because of this opportunity, with my parents help, I was able to purchase my first house in Tampa. By the time Les and I got married, he had a nice home to move into. It needed work, but he and I both had the skills and the desire to fix it up. We had quite a few animals, including two snakes, two large Dobermans, an iguana and an adorable little mutt. I loved my animals, especially the dogs as if they were children and so did Les. It was one of the things I loved so much about him. Solomon was the largest of the three dogs and had been left to me in a will, by my best friend, Patrick, who had died two years earlier. Solomon had a bit of a hard time with Les because he was jealous, but Les eventually won him over. The two girls, Sheba and Babbitt, were happy to have the attention from him because Solomon normally hogged so much of my time. All the dogs were treated equally of course, but truth be told, I felt so bad for Solomon, because he lost Patrick, I probably did give him the most attention. "Iggy" the iguana also loved to have attention and actually socialized with the dogs. When people would come to the door, the dogs and Iggy would all run to see who it was. Sometimes people were leery of entering, but once they came in, all the animals were quite friendly. Our home was warm and filled with love.

As suspected, I was pregnant and was walking on air the day I found out. I could not wait to tell Les when he arrived home. He seemed tired but had a big smile. I guess my hormones got the best of me because I didn't really feel his happiness as I thought I would. I figured it was my imagination.

During these months, I had an opportunity to visit with Les' family and my parents as well. Everyone was looking forward to the baby. Pam was a weirdo but she was a baby person, and although she had other grandchildren, she was excited about ours.

My parents were super excited about their first grandchild and flew to Florida to help us do some work on our home. It was a two-bedroom house, but Les and my dad split the second room and made a third bedroom. The smaller room became the baby's room. The spare room was filled to the brim with all the stuff people bought us for the baby. My parents were especially generous, furnishing the room with a crib and dresser and changing table. Now, it just needed a little paint and we could properly set up the baby's room. Les appreciated the help my dad gave him and told him that from this point forward, he wanted my dad to rest and relax. He assured my dad that he would finish painting after they left. During the rest of the week, we had a great time just catching up and enjoying my parents.

In those days, a sonogram was just a "blob" on the page. No fancy three-dimensional pictures, just a black blob. But during my appointment that day, when they put that little picture in my hands, that blob was the most beautiful thing I had ever seen in my entire life. In the pre-cell-phone days, I could not send the picture or post it anywhere, so I put it in my purse and started the drive home. I remembered that Les was trimming trees in a particular area, so I drove over to the site to see if I could show him the sonogram. In hindsight, he surely should have been at that doctor's appointment with me. Still, no red flags went up, because we both wanted to be able to take time off work once the baby was born. So we worked at much as possible.

When I arrived at Les' jobsite, he was having lunch with his buddies. He seemed happy to see me, but he did not stop to introduce me to any of his work friends and instead kind of pushed me off to the side to ask if everything was OK. I showed him the picture, and I knew he wasn't as excited as I was. I could feel a lump in my throat and started to cry. Les assured me that he was excited, just surprised to see me. I now know that his behavior was completely unusual for a first-time dad. He should have been grabbing the picture from my hand and showing all his work friends. Nothing like that happened, and I left with an empty feeling.

I knew his mom loved babies more than anything else in the world. I had watched her be a wonderful grandmother to Lydia's kids, so I decided to stop over and show her and Stan the picture. It was worth my while because she and Stan were yelling and screaming—exactly the reaction I had hoped for. When I returned home, I called my parents and told them about the sonogram. They also shouted through the phone with the joy of typical grandparents. The next call was my brother who was very excited and happy for us too . By the time I called Lydia and Vivvy, they already knew. Pam had called them because she just could not wait to tell someone. I laughed and thought that this was wonderful. I was floating on air again and stuck the sonogram to the fridge with a magnet.

When Les got home from work, I wanted to have a chat with him. I was upset over his behavior that day. He sat down, and I brought the picture to the table. He poked fun at the picture. He could not believe anyone could get excited about a blob on a paper. He wondered, "Where was this baby that everyone else could see?" He kept pointing and asking me, "What am I looking at here?" I remember crying and thinking he was a jerk that night. But after a satisfying dinner, a shower, and a good night's sleep, he was happy in the morning and making us breakfast and chatting on about the baby's room and the last thing left to do, which was to paint. I could feel my spirit lifting.

Anyone who knows me could tell you that on occasion I have a sixth sense about things. Although the sonogram could not detect whether we were having a boy or girl, I knew and felt that it was a girl. I wanted a pink room, period. Les did not agree and brought up points that if it was a boy, he didn't want his son in a pink room. We agreed on a darker lavender shade. As luck would have it, the paint dried on the wall and it was pink. This to me was a sign. To him, it was aggravation, and he talked about repainting the walls. He never got around to that, and the baby's room remained pink.

I had to start babyproofing my house as we were only about three months away at this point. I had to give away my two reptiles because I could not take the chance with a new baby. I found great homes for the boa and the python but was depressed about having to give them up. I still had the three dogs, and that was a great comfort to me. I was still working full time, and the people at my job were an amazing support system that I wanted to work until the last possible minute. I took my maternity leave on a Friday and the crew at work surprised me with a beautiful baby shower luncheon, with plenty of decorations, food and gifts. I was so overwhelmed with their kindness and I didn't want to leave, but I was so excited to start the next "page" in my life. I thanked them all and gave kisses and hugs around, promising to bring the baby in for a visit as soon as possible.

This was only four days away from my daughter's birthdate, so I didn't have much time at home, which was fine with me. All through my pregnancy, I craved oranges. I was eating anywhere from six to twelve on any given day. This caused me to have terrible heartburn, but I could not stop. Now that I was home, I was eating oranges all day. I had insane heartburn all day, every day. In addition, I was asthmatic and the baby was so heavy on my lungs, I had a hard time breathing, especially laying down on my back. So, I mostly sat up in a chair in the yard, or walked around the yard, so that I could be with the dogs. I no longer felt safe to drive, which was totally fine because we were down to one car at this point. My old car had died, and Les was driving a refurbished Mercedes-Benz that my parents had bought him for his birthday. It needed some work but he could fix anything. He did all the work on it himself, so he got to know all the neighbors from being outside so much. They would stop over to see how he was making out on the car. They also were starting to ask him about the baby and told him if we needed anything they would be there for us. It was comforting to have so many people who cared, since my entire family lived in New York.

On a Tuesday morning in July, I woke up with a backache. I had never felt anything like it in my life. This was my brother's birthday, and I picked up the phone to call him. I mentioned the backache, and he told me if it continued more than an hour to call my doctor. I mentioned how odd it would be if my baby would be born today, on his birthday. He agreed. I sang "Happy Birthday" to him and he thanked me and we said goodbye. As I stood to hang up the phone, blood and a clear substance ran down my leg. I immediately called my doctor. The medical people told me that this was normal and the baby could be born at any time within the next forty-eight hours. Within minutes, the back pain increased to the point where I couldn't stand comfortably, and I told Les not to leave for work. I told him we had to go to the hospital. He ran and got my bag, and we left. We were only about twenty minutes away, but the traffic was backed up for miles. I could feel an urge to push and instinct told me that if we didn't hurry, I would be having this baby in the car. We got to the hospital and told the receptionist how I was feeling. She immediately got a wheelchair and helped me to sit. Then she whisked me off toward a long hallway. We were at a nurse's station and there were three or four of them behind the desk. I told the nurse that I was having a baby right *now*. She argued and told me that it was my first baby and I knew nothing. She told me that the hospital would examine me but if I had no legitimate labor pains, they would send me home because it would probably be a long while. She pointed out that because I was a first-time mother, I was mistaken about the timeframe. I told her about the pain in my back, but she ignored me. I sat there while she made a call and soon, I felt the baby's head starting to emerge.

I started screaming, and the nurse ran around the desk. I told her that I could feel the baby's head and she said something stupid like "Oh my God, the baby is here already." I was thinking at the time that I should report her later for being so nasty to a first-time mother. Little did I know that within a couple of days, the heartache would be so bad that I would never even remember her.

Lizzy was born at 12:39 p.m. in the hallway of Tampa General Hospital's Maternity Ward. We never even made it into the labor room. She was the most stunning, gorgeous baby I had ever laid eyes on. Luckily she was also healthy and a whopping nine-pound-fifteen-ounces. I was in love. They put me and Lizzy in a room and told me to rest. Les went to work, telling me that he wanted to finish this day out and the next so he could be home with us the rest of the week. Lizzy had one tiny complication and was born with jaundice. They assured me that it was very common and would pass quickly. They explained how she had to be put under the bilirubin lights for a day, but they told me I could bring her home that Thursday. Everyone was so excited. My parents planned to fly in on Friday night to see their first grandchild, and Les' family was due to come over then as well.

On Thursday morning, I got out of bed and took out the soft yellow outfit I had selected to dress the baby in. It would have been pink if I had my way, but to avoid an unnecessary argument, I chose yellow. It had little matching shoes and a hat. The outfit just about fit Lizzy because she was bigger than expected, and I laughed as I dressed her. I had never been happier in my entire life. Les was due to come pick us up around 10:00 a.m., but that time passed. I got worried as the time ticked away. I kept calling our house and Les' family as well. Nobody knew a thing. I got nervous thinking he had been in an accident, so I called the police. There were no reports of any accidents or trouble with Les. I decided to call my neighbor Randi, who worked with me.

When Randi picked up the phone, I didn't let her speak. I immediately said, "Randi, Les isn't here to pick me up. Have you seen him?" She said, "I saw him earlier today, but I figured he was still putting the baby's room together because there was a moving van in front of your house all morning." I was confused. I could not imagine what was happening. We weren't moving anything. I decided that Les was probably trying to surprise me with new furniture or something, but still I could not reach him.

I asked Randi if she could pick us up at the hospital. The staff had told me that if we were not checked out by 5:00 p.m., then we would have to stay another night. So Randi came for us. When we got to my home, the front door was closed but unlocked. The dogs were all there greeting me. I put the baby chair onto the table and asked Randi to watch it for me. I ran through the house. It looked emptier. I soon realized that everything Les owned was out of the house. He had moved out while I was in the hospital. My legs were like jelly and I felt faint. Randi told me to call his family and not to panic. She even suggested that maybe he had gotten a new place for us to live and was moving us in as a surprise. In my gut, I knew this wasn't true. None of my stuff was gone, it was only his. I called his family again, and nobody knew anything. They also sounded surprised and everyone was frantic. He never did come home that night. I called the Police and reported him missing. They told me he would have to be missing a full forty-eight hours before he was officially a missing person. Lizzy and I spent her first night home totally alone with the dogs surrounding us, and I was confused and heartsick. I had no idea what to think. I briefly thought to call my parents, but they would be here the next day anyway and I didn't have the strength to pick up the phone again. I was slipping away into some trance like state. Fortunately, Lizzy was there and I had to take care of her. Something inside me kept me vigilant to do so.

That was the longest night I could remember in a long time and I didn't sleep a wink. When the daylight came through the front window, I felt a ray of hope. I knew my parents would be in this house with me in a few hours and it was the only thing that kept me sane.

My parents called when they arrived and I told them that Les had to go to work and I didn't have a car to pick them up. They mentioned that they had plans to rent a car anyway and would be there shortly.

I sat and waited for them to arrive.

After what seemed an eternity, I saw a white car pull up in the driveway and my heart started to pound. They were here. My entire body got the shakes. I barely had the energy to go and greet them at the door. When I saw them, I ran hugged them both at once and started to cry uncontrollably. They said "oh, we are so happy to see you too", where is Lizzy?" I stepped back and my Mom recognized immediately that things were not right. She asked me if I was okay? They both asked "Where is Les?". He should have been home from work by now. I had to tell them I didn't know. They were shocked and started to ask a lot of questions, but I was too weak to answer. Their focus immediately shifted to Lizzy in her little infant seat. Although they were worried about me, they could not ignore this amazing brand new life. The both ran to the baby and were talking to her and greeting her. They were so happy. Soon, the story spilled out, even though I didn't know much. They shook their heads and looked at each other, having a hard time absorbing the words "moved out while I was in the hospital". What should have been the happiest day of our lives was overshadowed by the mystery of Les' sudden departure.

I remember nothing from those early days. I think I had a nervous breakdown of some sort. I know only that my mother took over the care of my infant and me. My dad took care of my dogs and my house. I remember hearing them calling a lot of people on the phone, but I was in bed and could not even rise. I lost the entire first week with Lizzy. To this day, I don't remember a minute of it. I guess this was nature's way of shielding me somehow. There were absolutely no thoughts going through my head. I was dead inside and I didn't care.

One day, my dad came into the bedroom and asked me to come into the living room. I somewhat snapped out of my trance because he sounded very serious. He had hired a private investigator, and they had found Les. He did not want to come home. He told the investigator to pass on the word that he was confused. He also said he would come to see me. He agreed to come the next day at 12:00 p.m. to talk.

My mother practically dressed me for this meeting. She did my hair, and at 12:00 p.m. on the dot, Les showed up. He honked the horn. He didn't even want to come inside and see his child. Like a robot, I walked in my trance-like state toward the car and got in. I couldn't tell you what my parents said as I left, or where Lizzy was. I was traumatized and totally out of it at this point.

In Florida, it takes only a few moments in any given place to drive to an isolated area. Les drove us down a street and pulled over the car. He slid toward me on the seat, and I was up against the passenger window. I had no idea what his intentions were but he looked completely angry and nothing like the man I loved.

He reached under the seat and pulled out a huge butcher knife and placed it to my throat. He told me, "You are *not* divorcing me until I decide what I am going to do. If you try, I will filet you and Lizzy like pieces of fish." I peed my pants in the car that day and was so hysterical that I could not answer. I tasted salty tears in my mouth, but was not even aware that I was crying. He put the knife away and drove. I don't remember the ride home, but I had only one thought. I kept thinking it over and over. Would I ever see Lizzy or my family again? That question got answered when I heard him shout "get out" and I snapped out of my thoughts.

We were in front of my home and he reached in front of me and pushed down the door handle. Once the door opened, he shoved me out. I literally fell on the ground, and felt the course driveway under my legs and arms. It sounds crazy, but the physical pain felt good. At least I could feel *something*.

He backed out really fast, leaving me there and I saw smoke and heard the car motor rev up. I laid there watching, but not feeling anything. I was definitely in the worst state of my emotional life. I was no longer scared, I wasn't worried, I wasn't anything. That "dead" feeling remained with me.

The next thing I remember was being in the house. My dad was calling the police, and my Mom was guiding me into the bathroom to shower and change my clothes. I looked in the mirror at some point and felt the hair stand up on my arms. Was that girl in the mirror me? *Could it really get any worse?* I thought.

It did get worse.

This part of the story ends horribly. My parents agreed to pay Les $5,000 to sign divorce papers through an attorney. None of us ever saw him again. My father and mother took leaves of absences from their jobs and stayed to pack up my house. The real-estate company that I worked for agreed to take care of everything regarding the sale of the house. Then we drove away and headed for New York.

The saddest part, which still cuts me up today, is that I could not take my dogs. I can still see them in my mind waiting at the fence, looking at me with hope in their eyes to take them as we drove away. As I write this, I still feel sick thinking about that moment and I still feel like crying.

My friend Beth had a daughter who took all three dogs to her home, which was on a large property. I could not bear ever again to even see a picture of them. I was at the lowest point of my life, and it should have been the happiest.

In the time span of about four days, I had lost my husband, my home, my dogs, and my job and went back to New York with my parents to heal. Thank goodness for them, because I have no idea how our lives would have turned out had they not taken us away. I would have lived in fear every moment, thinking about Les and that butcher knife.

Lizzy and I ended up having a wonderful, thriving life together. She never did want to meet her dad, even after the days of the Internet began. None of his family contacted me during those remaining days in Florida. They were baffled and felt embarrassed over what he had done to us. And, they had no answers for me. Pam, as if to explain it all away, pointed out to me that Les was adopted and therefore, she had no responsibility for him. I felt like she wanted me to stop calling.

After we were back in New York, I had horrible nightmares of Pam and Stan coming to kidnap Lizzy. These fears were unfounded but they were so real to me. Soon, I stopped calling them and none of them called us again either, not even to see how Lizzy was. I will never know what happened or why. As horrible as this story is, it is what made me and Lizzy the people we are today. We have lived in many places and have had fabulous experiences, and I have a closeness not many people have with their children. I am remarried and have a loving, wonderful husband and a total of five children. Life is beautiful.

The Moral: When you hit rock bottom, the only way to go is up.

8 ELIZABETH–THE SCARIEST LOSER

Working with the general public in any job can be a challenge. When I met Elizabeth, it changed the way I looked at every client/customer for the rest of my life.

My young daughter and I had moved around the country a bit and had been relocated to California for work. I was now a consultant and was working with personal computers and networks. My specialty was programming and these were the years that every company was romancing computer people. There was work everywhere. I felt like it was a golden opportunity for Lizzy and me to move around while she not yet in "big girl school". We experienced many new places and met so many wonderful people.

Kyle was also moving around the country with his jobs too. He was involved in exercising and opening new gyms. He had lived in Miami Beach and many places in Colorado at the same time my daughter and I were on the move. We were far away from each other but always close in our hearts and to this day remain friends. I missed him a lot during some of the trying times in my life but I now had my own daughter and our lives were taking new direction all the time.

Los Angeles was lovely, with perfect weather, every single day. Almost nightly, we went to the Pacific Coast Highway beach trail, Lizzy on her big wheel and me walking beside her. I worked very hard and Lizzy was happy in nursery school. We enjoyed the two years we spent there tremendously. I had a big family and some of them were also in California and we spent time with them most weekends and really enjoyed it. There was always a nagging feeling in my gut however, because I missed the most important family members, my Mom, my Dad and my brother who lived back East. I worried that Lizzy would grow up, not knowing them and we had always been such a close family.

I began to apply for jobs with the sole purpose of getting closer to my family back home. Being a consultant made it easy to cut ties and pick up in any new location because every company was looking for computer professionals. I was lucky enough to find work back East and within a few months we were on our way, this time to New Jersey.

Lizzy was going to enter a fantastic school system in the fall, and we had a nice place to live and life was good. We got to see my parents and brother quite often and that made our lives complete. The project I was on would be ending at the end of summer and I decided to hunt for a full time job with health benefits. There was no reason to continue consulting or moving any longer.

While scouring the local papers one weekend, I noticed a job opening at a local technical college, teaching computer programming classes to adults. Having many years of programming experience, I thought it sounded like something I should consider. Teaching had never occurred to me, but the position paid well and was close to my home. Best of all, the hours coincided with Lizzy's school schedule. I wouldn't be sacrificing any time with her at all.

At first, the job was a dream come true. I loved the people I worked with, and teaching computer classes was a breeze. In addition, the reward of helping people felt good. Even though I was being paid, it never felt like work to me. My first year was just amazing. I loved my students and loved the job. I was even asked to give a speech at graduation, and many parents, husbands, wives, and others came up to me afterward and told me that I was an inspiration to their loved ones. It felt wonderful.

The next semester began in late August. The school began taking on many more students who came with government subsidies for their tuition for various reasons. This particular class was big, and out of twenty-five students, five of them had issues that I could clearly detect. One had Tourette's syndrome and would shout out obscenities in class, another had an eating disorder and would bring food into class, eat it, and then run to the bathroom to throw it up. A third student had such a poor attention span that he could not absorb anything and even needed to be reminded that he was in a computer-programming class. He talked loudly to himself during class and said "OK, thank you" about two-hundred times per class. One of the students, Elizabeth, seemed stranger than the rest. She came into class each day with a book bag so heavy that she could barely lift it. She was about forty years old and wore flowered "granny" skirts with hiking boots. She would pair these skirts with plaid or patterned loud, colorful blouses, so nothing ever matched. Her hair was styled in long, blond braids reminiscent of the von Trapp kids from *The Sound of Music*. Her makeup was odd as well, and looked like she belonged in an old *Betty Davis* movie. I didn't give much thought to their oddities though, because programmers tend to think out of the box and this sometimes lends itself to brilliant code. During the first week of school, I already thought the year would be a challenge. Still, I was eager to start and get to know everyone.

I noticed that Elizabeth was high strung. She would get upset with herself when code did not work and would often dash out of the room and run top speed up and down the hallway. During the winter, when the heat in the building was on so high that it felt like a desert in Egypt, she wore gloves to class because her hands were always cold. Eventually, she cut the fingertips of the gloves off so she could type better, but I never saw her without the gloves. She would bang her gloved hands on her keyboard and showed total frustration when things did not go her way those first two weeks. There was so much insanity in class every day that it was hard to keep track. The eating-disorder student running in and out to puke, the Tourette's girl shouting out, and the attention-span guy yelling at himself when things didn't go well. I often sat at my desk and looked out over the class wondering where some of these people would work, if ever. In addition, I began to look for another job.

Two weeks into the semester, the dean of students had a staff meeting and informed all the teachers that each of us would have a mandatory task of being guidance counselors to a handful of students. This was an effort to be sure they were staying on target, happy with the school, etcetera. It was not something I looked forward to. I enjoyed having their technical problems in my hands, but programming in Basic was not a qualification to counsel students. In addition, I didn't want to get involved on a personal level with anyone from this bunch. The dean assured us that it would be quick and painless and that we would just have to ask five questions pertaining to their school experience, write down their answers, and send them away.

In my opinion, if you are putting teachers who are not qualified to counsel in charge of this, then the teachers should never counsel their own students. The school didn't see it that way. Of course, I ended up being the guidance counselor to the students with the most issues. The other teachers called my students the "nut jobs." It was sad, but I had to admit that as a group, they seemed that way. You just don't want that much personal information about people you need to teach. I don't think this is done in normal schools, but a private technical school for adults did not need to follow these rules. At the end of the day, it was made clear to all of us that it wasn't an option and anyone not on board could leave. I put my best foot forward and agreed to take on the ten or twelve students assigned to me.

My first meeting with three or four of the students went exactly as planned. They were as smooth, fast, and painless as the dean had assured us. I gained a false sense of security.

The next student on my list was Elizabeth. I had the five requisite questions ready to go. Elizabeth plopped her book bag onto the floor between us and slid her colorfully clad body into the chair in front of me. Out of my lips came the first question: "Elizabeth, how is your semester of school going overall?" Her reply: "Actually, school is not going very well. Since I killed my parents and have to come to school in a bus from the psychiatric center, people look at me differently, and it is hard to concentrate on schoolwork."

Immediately, I could feel the little hairs stand up on my arms and the back of my neck. I concentrated on having the most stoic expression I could muster as Elizabeth babbled on. I knew I appeared calm but inside, I was total jelly. I desperately searched my head for something, anything to say. Finally, I heard words coming from myself. "I am sorry to hear that, Elizabeth, but that was then, this is now. You are in school, and it is time to just move on and think about doing well here." She was pleased with this answer and continued to chatter away.

I examined her facial expressions as she spoke. Was it my imagination, or did she even look crazy? Nope, not my imagination—she looked like a psycho. Her big, bulgy eyes seemed to come unglued from their sockets, and her hands were shaking like someone with Parkinson's disease. She talked about the long list of drugs she took each day in order to reenter society. When she returned to the mental hospital each night, she was plied with drugs as well. I made a note on my pad: "look up Thorazine" as she iterated through her list.

I never did get to ask the remaining four questions because she never stopped talking. In addition, I was in a state of shock and forgot completely about the task at hand. Each moment that ticked by seemed like an hour. I was alone in a room with a girl who had killed her parents. The details flowed out of her mouth as if she were giving me a recipe.

She killed her parents in a car while they were driving. She had been in the back seat and was angry with them because she wanted to smoke a cigarette and they would not allow it. She reached into her purse and took out a hand gun and killed them both. My heart started to pound. Who even has a gun in their purse? She included details about how difficult it was to stop the car after she shot her dad, who was driving. Basically, she crawled over the seat, sat in her dad's lap, who was dying and brought the car to a halt. Her mother also lay bleeding but remained alive long enough to watch Elizabeth light up a cigarette. Elizabeth later confessed that it was a personal thrill to smoke while her mother watched and died. She claimed she needed to relax, and now she could smoke without any interference. She also said she was starving and had to figure out what to do for lunch. I looked at her smiling face, with her bulging eyes and Cheshire grin. I looked at the large, heavy book bag between us and wondered what was in it. I reminded myself to keep smiling and say positive things so she would also keep smiling until the meeting ended.

Immediately following this counseling session, I ran to the dean's office and walked in with no appointment. "So I have a murderer on my list of students to counsel?" The dean said, "How do you know she is a murderer?" Still, there was no shock on her face, and I knew immediately that the dean was fully aware of Elizabeth's past. She went on to talk about rehabilitation and how the government was funding her education. It was an eye-opener, but I assured her that I wanted nothing to do with the counseling of this girl. I explained that being a programmer was not the ideal skill set to process the thoughts of a cold-blooded killer. Although I had a psychology minor in school, it was something I chose not to practice in order to avoid situations like the one I was in. I told the dean I would remain Elizabeth's teacher but refused to counsel her any longer. I really should have given my notice that day because I no longer wanted to be in class with Elizabeth. Being a single mom, however, gave me absolutely no option but to remain with a steady paycheck until I could find something else. Also, we had security guards at the school, the other teachers now were aware of everything, and I relaxed a bit knowing that there were more sets of eyes on Elizabeth. Did I think she could be rehabilitated? Hell no.

From that point forward, Elizabeth made it known that she felt close to me, and each day she would flounce into the room and stop and hug me. Although I was not her counselor any longer, she continued to catch me before school, after school, and in the bathroom and reveal personal details about her parents, her life, and their deaths.

As far as her schoolwork and grades went, I am not proud to say this, but I never again truly graded any test or homework that Elizabeth handed in. I would simply pick up her paper, see her name on it, grab a pen, and mark a huge "A" at the top and write things like "Excellent Work" or "Way to Go" and add little smiley faces. On paper, Elizabeth was the smartest student in the school. She was still getting upset at her computer station and banging on the keys, crying during tests, and yelling at herself, but she was calmed by her grades and felt accomplished.

I knew Elizabeth would never be let out of the psych hospital to be released into any company for work. I knew she wouldn't ever be a corporate employee, let alone anyone's programmer. In the grand scheme of things, she was happy, and although I was constantly on edge, I had to get through a few more weeks of the semester.

Elizabeth continued to share elaborate fantasies. She mentioned that she possessed a third eye in the middle of her forehead and that Michael Jackson's song *Thriller* was about her. She said "Mikey" would one day marry her. She claimed he was mentioning her name as he sang "thriller, thriller, thriller." Upon listening to the song with my daughter that night, I could hear where the voice inflection sounded like her real name. (All names in this story have been changed.) She also spoke about aliens that crept into her hospital at night with drugs and sex for her, and without them, her life would be total shit. She had two brothers and had fantasies about them being proud of her for getting rid of their parents. Her delusions, although entertaining, sent messages to everyone that the girl was a ticking time bomb.

When I came into my classroom on my birthday that year, it had been decorated by students and teachers with balloons, crepe paper, and a beautiful cake on the desk. Everyone sang *Happy Birthday*. Once the festivities ended, Elizabeth came to me and whispered into my ear. She couldn't wait to tell me that her mother's birthday was also this day. There was something so eerie and creepy about it that I could not bear the thought of staying at the school for the next year. I gave my notice that day. I was lucky and got a new job that coincided with the end of the school year. I never burned bridges and didn't want to start then. I could not wait to get to my new job and put major distance between myself and this school.

A few weeks after graduation, I received a thick envelope in the mail. It was from Elizabeth. My heart pounded. How did she know where I lived, and what was she sending me? I can only assume something with my address was sitting in or on my desk that year and she was able to retrieve that information. The envelope contained a manuscript of her life, including her intricate thoughts. She saw herself as God and mentioned this in the book. She mentioned that her parents were deserving of death because of their sins. She also had written down her thoughts after the killing them, including her arrest that would eventually put her into the psychiatric hospital. I was holding her diary in my hands. I was in great fear and called the hospital to see how she could possibly have gotten my address and if she was still incarcerated. The hospital assured me that she was still there but gave me the news that she would be released to live in a halfway house within six months. I was scared to death and considered moving my daughter and myself out of the state. I went to the local police station and reported this and also told the mental hospital, just in case anything happened to us.

We lived in fear for a few weeks. Then, about a month later, our local news carried a story about Elizabeth and how she would return to the psych hospital for life because she had set the halfway house on fire, endangering everyone inside. Some people were treated for critical injury, but all survived. She will never be let out again, and to this day I watch the news for her parole hearings, in which she is always denied.

The Moral: If someone gives you job responsibilities that don't fit and threaten you to take that job or leave it, leave it. Get out before it gets worse, because it most certainly will.

9 DINA–THE "OLD SOCK" LOSER

Our friendship had survived nearly twenty years. Dina was my old sock, like the ones everyone has that are comfy and cozy but so old that they have holes and other flaws. You cannot seem to part with them because of the comfort that they have given you. That moment you stand over the garbage and finally toss them away hurts. Unlike the throwaway sock, in the end, Dina cut me loose.

I met Dina at a nail salon during a biweekly appointment. She was approximately forty-five years old at the time, and we had commonality. During our concurrent nail appointments, we shared ideas, recipes, and other life topics over the next three or four years. I looked forward to getting my nails done because of her, and our friendship deepened. We laughed, we cried, and we were just girls having fun. It was refreshing to meet someone who had that kind of commonality, and Dina made me smile whenever I thought about her.

Before long, Dina invited me to her house to meet her cats. It was this day that I realized she was different and had issues. Dina was a never-been-married woman who was independent enough to be a homeowner. I was eager to see her place, and being an animal person, I was looking forward to meeting the kitties.

I walked in and was not surprised by the cat smell. I was shocked, however, to see that the condo was a cluttered shit hole. Things were stacked everywhere. There was absolutely nowhere to sit, and everything had a visible layer of cat fur at least an inch thick. I found this to be surprising from a single older woman with no children. Living alone would give her an opportunity to clean up, wouldn't it? My house was a wreck, but I had kids and a full-time job, a big dog and many small animals, and still my house looked like a palace comparatively. I pictured those poor souls on a TV show where they showcase people who hoard things. Still, Dina was my friend, so I ignored the shit storm around us and just settled in on the floor.

As we chatted, she entertained me with stories about each cat and its individual personality, and I just loved it. Also, the cats could perform some tricks. They were so adorable that I was truly enjoying myself. Next, she asked if I would like to see pictures of her deceased mom and dad. I knew they had been dead for some time and that she missed them terribly. She had one sibling, a sister she barely spoke to. I took this as a gesture of letting me in to share her life with me.

She asked me to accompany her to her bedroom because she kept their pictures in her "underwear drawer". It seemed strange when she said this, but she was a unique person and I trusted her, so I simply nodded and followed her down the hall. When we got to her room, she opened the underwear drawer and pulled out a tiny photo album and handed it to me. I sat on the bed and opened the book. In every single picture, her parents were dead. They were lying in their caskets, and there were follow-up pictures of their graves. My unfiltered response: "What the *fuck*, Dina, are you sick in the head? Of all the pictures you can show me, you choose dead-people pictures?" She just laughed and told me I was overreacting and said she was comforted by the pictures. I thought she was a sick bitch, but I wasn't scared of her; in fact, she was a source of fascination to me. The girl was obsessed with death, so what?

I remember speaking to Kyle about this and his reaction was that she sounded like some of the "weirdos" we had encountered in Florida. He told me to be careful. We had been through so much together, we were actually starting to smarten up a bit. I agreed, but aside from her weird, personal life at home, I had no nagging, negative feelings about her. But, I also had no idea how truly weird she was at that point either.

One afternoon, Dina came to our house with a box of empty holy cards. She was having a hard time trying to decide what she should write on them for her funeral, which was completely planned and had been for years. Her grave site and gravestone were already purchased and half chiseled in. She expressed to us that the only thing missing was her "death date." She had her music, Pachelbel, picked out for her procession at the church. She was Catholic and mentioned that all her people would have to sit through a long service, but it was something they would not forget. Dina was a character, but she had grown to be my friend. I accepted her weird, interesting traits.

Another of Dina's quirks was her addiction to tanning. She would sit in the sun from sunrise to sunset and even endured scabs and blisters in order to achieve her perfect tan. The tan looked absolutely awful on her, but she thought it was beautiful. Her skin was the color of black dog fur. People stared at her as they tried to guess her race. We told her over and again that the tan was too dark and that she would die from skin cancer. She just laughed all of it off. Perhaps she was trying to get to her funeral sooner.

Dina's spin on things was hilarious and so different from our own that she made every visit fun. Since she was an animal person, she paid attention to all of our pets, especially our dog, Samson. One day, "Sammy" came into the house from the yard with some kind of object in his mouth that resembled a stick. He jumped onto the couch next to Dina and spit the object onto her chest. We quickly found out it was a slug. Dina weighed approximately 350 pounds and was short, but I have never seen a human jump and run so fast. She did a little dance in the living room to try to shake off the slug. The entire time, our 160-pound Rottweiler was jumping around her and barking. After all, he loved her so much that he was just trying to share his "toy." The dance made it the ultimate fun day for him. We coined that experience as "Dina's Slug Dance" and still talk about it to this day.

Dina came to our house every Sunday afternoon. In addition to cooking for her, entertaining her, and putting music on her iPod, I listened and kept all of her deepest, darkest thoughts and secrets. I began to see red flags and detected a mean streak in her, but she was never mean to me or my family, so I didn't focus on it. She told a story about a former live-in boyfriend named Lenny. Apparently, he was flirting with a girl they both knew. She waited to get him into bed that night, and upon giving him a blow job, she bit him as hard as she could. As he writhed in pain, she said that if she discovered that he ever cheated on her, then she would "bite it off" and he wouldn't get away so easily. This story sent up a huge red flag, but they say that all is fair in love and war, and I just accepted what she told me and filed it away in my memory.

Everyone in my household and my immediate family became close with her through the years. Before long, everyone was doing things for Dina. My husband changed all screens and filters at her home, fixed things, and even laid new tile at no charge. We took turns going to her house and brushing the snow off her car. We took care of her cats when she wasn't home and helped her with all of her technology needs for work. She asked us to take her shopping from time to time because she didn't like parking lots and traffic. She complained about her weight and how she didn't feel steady in parking lots and felt like she needed an arm from time to time. We all took care of Dina because she was alone and we loved her. At the time, we didn't feel she was taking advantage because she was one of us.

Then life as we knew it with Dina changed. She opted for gastric bypass surgery to lose weight. She was heavy, but she was beautiful to me and I thought it was extreme. She wore a mask to bed at night in order to treat her sleep apnea and insisted the surgery would improve the quality of her life. Also, there was an ulterior motive for this surgery that she did not share this with us at the time.

Once Dina got the surgery, her personality changed. She would visit and strategically place herself in a chair where she could view her reflection in our mirrored cabinet. She would stare at herself the entire time we ate, chatted, or played games. She became conceited and did nothing but talk about herself and how beautiful people thought she was now. She was still at least 150 pounds overweight, but she was enamored with herself. It became painful to hold conversations with her.

In addition, Dina became obsessed with Andrew, a man at work who was at least thirty years younger. She revealed to us that her surgery was her first step to attracting him. She was delusional. Her conversations about him became X-rated and made us uncomfortable. She stopped at nothing and did not care who was in the room listening. Each time Dina visited, I had to make sure my youngest daughter was not in earshot of these stories. We were also sick of hearing them and put them into the "too much information" category.

From what we could tell, this boy gave her no encouragement whatsoever and in fact lived with a beautiful girl whom he planned to marry. This didn't stop Dina. She became so obsessed and jealous that she planned their breakup and fantasized about it constantly. Anyone who flirted with Andrew at work immediately made her "shit list," and she would tattle on them for any wrongdoing. She would brag about that to us. She acted as if Andrew was her property. We were shocked to find out that she even made him executor of her will just to obligate him and to reel him in. We commented negatively about these actions, but she took no notice of anything we said. Conversations for hours on end focused on Andrew. We finally saw less and less of Dina because it became so boring to listen endlessly about what Andrew wore and how his "package" looked in his tight pants or how she wished she could lick food off his body. There was no reasoning with her. She didn't think these conversations were sick in any way.

Because Dina was alone in life, we felt sorry for her and continued to invite her for holidays. I could no longer mix her with normal people, though, so she came to events that only my immediate family attended. They were all sick of her but were used to her ways. Everyone just tuned her out.

One year, everything changed. Jon, who worked for a local plumber, went to her house to perform some maintenance on her water heater. She told me that after this service, she trapped him at the front door and told him he could not leave without a kiss good-bye. As the details of her story unfolded, I was shocked to learn that she ended up having sex with him in her living room among the clutter and cat fur. What kind of person must he be? Then again, we thought they would be a perfect classless match. At least Jon was an adult. A bonus was that her conversations about Andrew came to a halt as her focus turned to Jon.

She told us that Jon looked like a well-built Santa Claus. He had a long white beard and a beautiful body. He was approximately her age, and they spent the next year at her house in bed. She once came to our house and had a pornographic picture of them she wanted to show us. We were not interested, and she just laughed it off. She didn't come over much anymore, but when she did, she shared all the gory details of their sex life. She was like an unpaid prostitute. We also found out that Jon was married but separated from his wife and headed for divorce. Her stories were like porn, and I was constantly trying to change the subject because it made me and my husband uncomfortable. Gone were any chats about work, recipes, our animals, or anything else. The irony is that she considered herself a strict Catholic and made jokes about how she would run to church for forgiveness after having sex with a married man. Our Sunday afternoons with her became boring and obligational. In addition, she would RSVP "yes" to parties and then never call or show up. She had turned into a horrible friend.

The final blow was the day my eldest daughter got married. Dina was a no-show, and my entire family worried about her, taking away from this beautiful affair. When the wedding weekend was over, we heard some feeble excuse on the answering machine. We all gathered around and listened and found it to be a bullshit excuse. We all knew she took an opportunity to have sex with Jon instead of attending the wedding.

She did attend our Christmas party that year, but at that point I was done with her. When she came to the door, I felt none of the usual emotional attachment.

This party turned out to be the last time she entered our home. It was the worst Christmas I can remember because of Dina and her filthy mouth and inappropriate stories. I had to pull her into the kitchen several times and explain that my seventy-five-year-old mother and fourteen-year-old daughter were embarrassed and she should think about leaving if she could not control herself.

The last straw happened when my newly married daughter arrived. She hugged Dina and said, "How have you been?" This was the perfect time for Dina to apologize for missing the wedding. Instead, Dina replied, "How do you think I am? I am a mess; I am dating a married man." As always, everything was about Dina. She also told us in the kitchen that day that dating a married man had its advantages. She said that "if he steps out of line even a little bit, she would not hesitate to call wifey and tell her everything." At that moment, my daughter and I looked at each other and a mental note passed between us. We realized that our relationship with Dina was finished.

Being an outspoken person, I would naturally be the one to just tell her off and cut her out of our lives forever. Instead, I said nothing. Twenty years of friendship with Dina had softened me. Anyone else in my life would have been cut out swiftly and forever.

About two weeks after Christmas, my husband and I were sitting in the living room one evening when the phone rang. The caller was asking questions about Dina and Jon. Apparently, Jon was a liar, a cheater, and not separated or divorced. He was part of a loving family that we got to know pretty well that weekend. They expressed their need to get to the bottom of Jon's relationship with Dina. Jon's wife was about to enter chemotherapy for cancer. We had no idea how they found us, and we didn't ask. They called several times that week. At first, we told them nothing because we had not spoken to Dina. I tried to call and email her, and she did not reply.

Finally, my husband and I made a moral decision to help this family in any way we could. We furnished any and all information we had, which was not much because we didn't know Jon except through Dina's stories. They were able to piece together schedules and timings that made sense to them, and they thanked us for our help. They also mentioned that Dina was just one in a long list of whores in Jon's life. The women all knew that he was married and continued to have relationships with him. In the end, the family just wanted their mother to concentrate on her health and throw Jon out. They just needed the proof to present to her, which they got from several families just like ours. How all of that turned out, we will never know. We never spoke to them about it again. We occasionally comment on Facebook to each other but their family is still healing. Luckily, the mother's cancer is in remission and they just want to focus on the good now. The most significant thing is that we never heard from Dina, ever again, despite our many attempts to contact her so that we could tell her how we felt. She had cut the entire family out.

Two years went by, and my youngest daughter and I were coming out of the bathroom at a local department store. We found ourselves face-to-face with Dina. When she saw how close to her we were and recognized who we were, she turned on a dime and ran out of the store as fast as her fat little legs could carry her. I never realized what a coward she was until that moment.

It is still incredible to me that Dina changed so much through the years and the horror that she became. But the fact that she would rather be home performing sex acts on her loser, married boyfriend instead of attending my daughter's wedding was too much to bear. And that she lied about it. She is a cowardly, hypocritical, self-absorbed loser who cut me out. And that is the one thing about her that I am eternally grateful for.

The Moral: When a friendship becomes a one-way street, it's time to cut your losses. Or you can stop catering to the loser because he or she will surely cut you out before you have a chance.

10 BESSIE–THE BLOOD-CLOT LOSER

You cannot pick your family. I never thought I would be the kind of person to turn my back on a family member. Yet, thinking back, the only mistake I made was not doing it sooner. My husband, Ken, made the decision to cut out this loser because he knew she was on a path to ruin our lives together. It was Bessie's core position in the family that kept her in our circle for so long. It was also her core position that allowed her to cause irrevocable damage that would affect every member in our little family in the end. It also affected our relationships with Ken's family. We would never be a whole unit again thanks to this loser. People don't have a right to use their hierarchy in a family to take power over other people, but this is where Bessie's story begins.

Bessie is my husband's mother, who lives in in another country. Some of the differences we had with her could be explained as a cultural divide. Other differences could be explained as classic in-law rivalry, but overall, we have in-laws in the family who are still dear to us and we have no issues with them. The truth unveiled itself, but it took many years. We realized that the very person who should want everyone to get along has a warped sense of what family is. She is the divide in the family. She enjoyed her children holding her in high esteem and doing her bidding. At the same time, she did not want them to get along with one another. It was much easier for the kids to just let everything she said go in one ear and out the other rather to confront her about it. They grew up in this environment, so it was their "normal." In her sick mind, this was how she held power over them. Then, when someone comes along from a normal family, this sick behavior sticks out like a sore thumb and dealing with it is disturbing. I liken it to a Stockholm syndrome, when your captor becomes the one you defend.

Ken and I have a blended family of five children. Their ages at the time we met went from nineteen all the way down to four. It is sometimes a difficult task to blend families, but when you are initially separated by an ocean, it makes the task harder. We introduced the kids through the use of phone calls and webcams. We instilled an attitude into all of them that all they needed to do was open their minds to the love, and the rest would happen naturally. We were looking forward to that first summer with a nice long vacation. We would be together day and night and begin to grow as a family. I had always wanted a big family, and not only did the man of my dreams walk into my life, but he also had children in tow. I could not be happier.

It so happened that we needed to arrange a chaperone at some point to bring two of the children (twins) onto the airplane to the US for the summer because they were younger than twelve. Since Bessie was retired, my husband thought of her immediately. We thought it would be amazing for the kids to bond not only with each other, but with their grandmother too. She lived far from them and had no license or car, so we thought it would be a treat for her. Ken was excited to call his mom and invite her to America with the main goal of bringing the twins to us. She had never been abroad, and we wanted to take her everywhere, treat her to everything, and relax and bond with us. We had so many plans for family fun.

The phone call did not go well. Bessie immediately took a defensive posture and laid into my husband, claiming his intent was to get her to babysit all the kids for us. She further stated that she would not be used for this purpose. She followed up her speech by slamming down the phone. It was shocking to me because not only had I never met this woman, but I also was used to a mom who would do anything to have her family together. My mother would swim over an ocean with the opportunity to be with her grandchildren. I should mention that money was not an issue because Ken and I were paying for every single thing, including her entertainment once she got here. I was stunned but didn't want to upset Ken, so I said nothing. I figured he knew how to handle his family.

We were truly in a pickle. Plans had been made, tickets for the twins had been purchased; what would we do next? Ken has a lovely sister Lena. He decided to call her for help. She was delighted, and I got an instant happy feeling from her over the phone. We all laughed and were excited and looking forward to this time together. I couldn't wait to meet and bond with my new sister.

When a phone rings, it always has the same tone. However, there are times in my life that when a phone rings that I just feel there is bad news waiting for me at the other end. I felt this horrible feeling in the pit of my stomach, unaware that there would be hundreds of times like it through the next five years.

"Hello?" was all I said. Bessie was at the other end shouting, asking me why I was causing trouble in the family. I was shocked and confused to say the least. I had no idea why she was angry, and I had no idea how someone I never even met could be so mean to me for no reason. I handed the phone to Ken. I heard him talking about Lena coming, and I heard him sputtering a word here or there when he could get one in, but I had no idea what was being said on the other end. Ken mentioned to her that he had called her first, and he reminded her that she had turned down this offer. I could see a change in his demeanor. Once he got off the phone, he explained that his mother was angry at us for inviting Lena over and not her. I asked him to repeat this because it made no sense. He mentioned that his mom had horrible mood swings and that I would get used to her and her ways. I was shocked and asked about Lena. Ken said, "I think she will still come." Before I knew it, both Bessie and Lena were going to chaperone the kids and both were coming for a nice visit. I was thrilled to have my new mom and sister coming so I could get to know them. I was too busy and happy to focus on the weirdness of that phone call, so we just dropped it and moved on.

The trip was nothing short of a nightmare. I felt crazy. Bessie was the most unstable, irrational human I had ever met. And now she was family to me. I could not understand how she was the person who raised my husband and Lena. She had horrible bouts of anger that made her face turn to stone, which scared our kids. I likened her temper tantrums to that of a two-year-old whenever she didn't get her way. Everything upset her, scared her, made her mad, and I had never met a more negative, unreasonable person in my life. Now I was stuck with her in my home for weeks to come. This was supposed to be the most special time ever for our new family to bond, and she was ruining it. We spent not one day of happiness during that time. Ken, Lena, our children, and I walked around on eggshells. Even tickets to Broadway and dinners out in New York City seemed to infuriate her. She spent most of those times with her arms crossed and lips pursed and refusing to speak to anyone. It was a lot to take in when we had five children to entertain on our only precious weeks off work.

My husband was not initially bothered by it. Having grown up with her, he was used to her crankiness and told me that he just blocked it all out. My sister-in-law, however, was empathetic and told me that some people should be kept at arm's length until you know how to cope with them. This coming from her eldest daughter seemed a bit strange, but I knew Lena to be a solid, upstanding person who never lied. And she had been there to witness all that I had, so I knew she was only looking out for me. She was elegant and classy about it. She wasn't pointing fingers, she wasn't saying anything mean or negative, and she was just telling me to take it slow and to watch and listen. She was giving me advice because she and I bonded instantly, and she didn't want to see me hurt. I made a mental note to stay on guard.

The next day, Mum was taking a shower. Lena and I were both "corporate girls" in the sense that we worked full-time, forty-hour weeks and enjoyed our jobs. While Mum was in the shower, I offered to take Lena to my company and give her a tour. The campus was huge, and the tour would have been about a five-mile walk. Mum's feet were still completely torn up from walking around New York in sandals the day before. We tried to tell her to wear comfortable shoes, but she would not have it. I guess it would have given her less to complain about. Anyway, Lena and I kissed Ken and promised to be back soon. When we got home, Bessie was in the garden in her typical horrible mood, furious with me because I had taken Lena to my office and not invited her. She was a coward and did not come to me with this information. Instead, we learned about it later when Ken told us that she had said, "When they come home, I will have her for this." I couldn't believe my ears. Ken pointed out that her feet were torn up and that she would have no interest in this five-mile walk through a corporation. It just gave her fuel for the rest of the day to be a jerk. We had a day planned with the kids, and it was ruined. Bessie refused to leave the house, and nobody got to go anywhere. My eldest son was upset with her and told her, and she had a huge falling-out with him. From that moment on, he stayed glued to his room and/or his computer and didn't socialize with anyone.

Things continued this way through the rest of the vacation. Nobody except for Bessie enjoyed anything. She fully enjoyed the fighting, the arguing, and the chaos. Just to round things up, when the twins had arrived on the plane from England , they had hundreds of little friends in their hair in the form of nits and lice. We didn't catch this while they were in the house, but the kids on this side of the ocean and I were loaded with them once the twins left. We called Lena and told her what had happened. What a way to end an already horrible visit. We spent the entire weekend washing and combing nits out of everyone's heads, washing sheets, pillows, clothing, brushes, etcetera. I found myself longing to go back to work. The sooner this vacation was at an end, the better.

Still, I chalked it up to so much happening at once. Sometimes things just start out bad and get worse, and you just have to let it go.

Through the years, Bessie came to visit on her own. She came for three months at a time, twice a year. Added together, it amounts to six months out of a year. Half of every year was wasted on trying to please this woman. I wish I knew then what I most certainly know now because I would never even try to please her. She cannot *be* pleased.

Ken and I had problems, but all of them boiled down to her. If we were having a discussion behind closed doors, she would listen outside the door and later give her opinion. She mentioned that she did not like the way I spoke to her son. She picked away at little things and made them big things, especially with the kids. She would have the sweetest face on, and the minute my husband left the room, she would look at me with hate. Before long, we felt uncomfortable in our own house. We all wondered what we were doing wrong to make Nanny unhappy and causing her to react this way. What did I know? She cannot be happy unless she poses herself as the victim and has everyone catering to her.

Ken owned a business and spent much more time at home than I did. I could not wait to go to my nine-to-five job each day. I figured Ken was used to his Mum and I wasn't, so I felt free once I was in my car every morning, away from her. What I didn't know was that she spent every waking moment with Ken, trying to poison his mind against me, my kids, my family, and America. When I got home in the evenings, not only did I have to contend with cooking for everyone, but I also had to have long conversations with Ken so he could tell me about what his Mom was saying. It was ridiculous. Basically, I had to justify why I lived and breathed. My husband's thinking was muddled. He could not focus or concentrate. She didn't give him a minute's peace during any given day.

Not only did we pay all her expenses when she was with us, but we also paid all her bills at home while she was visiting. She had everything she wanted from food to clothing to hair-dressing appointments to cigarettes and liquor. We made sure she was treated like a queen, but that still wasn't good enough for her.

During her semiannual visits, she was never asked to cook, clean, or babysit. But on one occasion, Ken and I were running late and Bessie was "stuck" with our five-year-old daughter for an hour. When I came home, Bessie was sitting in our green rocker with her famous stone face and crossed arms. I asked what had happened. She informed me that my daughter was spoiled and ill-mannered and that she owed her Nanny an apology. I went up to my daughter's room, closed the door, and asked her to tell me what had happened. My daughter burst into tears and told me she was afraid of Nanny and begged me never to be left alone with her again. She said that Bessie was mean to her the minute she walked in the door and put her little book bag down. Nanny told her it was "too bad" that she was hungry and would not allow her to spoil her dinner with a snack. She also would not allow her to play outside with her best friend, even though we had planned that activity over the phone when I knew I would be late. I will never know exactly what took place that day, but I do know that my youngest daughter handled it with more maturity than my mother-in-law ever could. I told my daughter that she was a good little girl and not to worry. She had my promise never to be left alone with Nanny again; however, I also asked her to apologize to Nanny simply to make Daddy happy. I would protect her no matter what, and she was so smart that she understood we were just going through the motions during this apology. She knew she had done nothing wrong. We both went downstairs, and she apologized for anything she may have said wrong, and I apologized for all the troubles we just went through. In hindsight, I shouldn't have. I did it to keep the peace, but I soon realized that Ken and all his siblings had been doing that for years. All of them were familiar with her and her ways, but they just swept it all under the rug in order to avoid conflict with her. None of them was familiar with talking things out. This took a mental toll on all of them and left them with issues they will live with forever.

We noticed a pattern starting to emerge. We noticed that she talked about everyone in the family. She didn't have a good thing to say about anyone, not even the children and babies. I had never met them but wondered what kind of a family I had married into. Ken has four siblings, and his mother would run them and their children into the ground during normal dinner conversation. She told us all their problems and their issues and how good it was to be away from it. Funny thing was, at the time, we got along with all the siblings. I never met any of them face-to-face except for Lena, but we enjoyed conversations over the phone and by webcam with all but one sister, whom I had never spoken to.

Eventually, all but Lena seemed cold to us. We could not put our finger on it. It took us a long time to realize that she had been going back home and talking about us, in particular me. Where she could not find negative things to say, she just made up stuff. We had people in the family who shared with us what she had said. She told them that she had suffered emotional abuse here. She said it was mainly my fault but that Ken went along with anything I said. Yet she continued to come and denied that she had said these things. She had successfully throughout the period of a year turned each sibling against the other. I became the "bad guy" even though I had always treated her with the respect that a mother deserved. Looking back, I realized I had done too much for her. I treated her like a queen, and she took that to heart. Of course, all of this was my opinion and how I felt inside. Ken and my kids felt this way too.

I could feel myself getting sick to my stomach weeks before each visit. I could not put this on my husband. He had left his entire family for me. I could not now suggest keeping this woman away. I just couldn't see how things could get worse. She was so manipulative. She could look at my face and say the sweetest things to me, and when I went to work, she talked shit about me to my own husband.

Since Ken had grown up with her, he was used to a house divided. He had no idea that any of this was bad, and it took him years to see it all.

In August of the next year, Mum was leaving and wanted to plan her next visit to America before she left. She thought that it would be great to come in January. I mentioned that there might be a few complications with this time and suggested she come toward the end of March or in April. She wanted to know why. I explained that winter would be upon us. It gets cold in her part of the world, but I could guarantee she never saw snow like she would see here. I know she doesn't like the cold, and I could not imagine anyone wanting to go somewhere with disagreeable weather. The second and bigger issue was that March 4 would be our anniversary. Unbeknownst to Ken, I had planned a weekend away for just the two of us in the city. I had purchased Broadway tickets to see *Spamalot*. I knew he would love the humor and the weekend away. I mentioned to her that if she came to us early, we would still be going through with our plans.

She specifically told us that it would be no problem at all for her and she would be there for three months, so what was one weekend away? She also mentioned that she could help with our youngest daughter.

There was no way I would put any of our children into a situation ever again where they would need to be alone with Nanny. So we compromised. We booked her tickets to arrive in February and leave in April; however, we also planned for our eldest daughter to stay at home that weekend with Nanny and our youngest daughter. We made dinner reservations for Bessie and the kids to go to a beautiful steak house for dinner, and we left them $500 to pay for it. We asked our daughter to take Nanny and her sister to a nice movie afterward and to breakfast the next morning.

Bessie arrived in February and immediately went to work on my husband. Within one week, I could see my husband looking at me out of the corner of his eyes in disgust. His treatment of me became just awful. I could not wait to get away. The weekend arrived, and the entire time we were in New York trying to enjoy our special celebration, Ken treated me horribly. He finally confessed that he wasn't sure he even wanted to remain in America. She had gotten to him, and she had done her job well. Ken resented me, my kids, and America in general. Since I love my husband, I would never want him to be trapped anywhere. I want his total happiness, even if that meant he would move back home with his Mum. I mentioned this and told him to think it over. He could let me know what he had decided sometime before she would depart.

When we arrived home on the train, we had a much bigger problem to contend with. Bessie was in the green rocker again, in her mood, but this time was rocking back and forth like someone with a severe mental disorder. Ken didn't want to speak to her at all. In his mind, he was already furious with me and didn't want to upset his mother as well. I went into the living room, and she began to spout hateful things at me. Talking about how we abandoned her in a strange country. How could we do this to her, taking off to the city and leaving her alone, hungry, and scared? At that moment, I knew she was either a complete sicko or she was the best manipulator I had ever seen. I had some psychology training in my background, and she was like a problem that needed to be fixed. She was like a science project gone wrong.

She shared with me that she wanted to go home right then. So Ken and I paid for her early return flight home and drove her to the airport. Ken had decided she was a kook and he was better off in the States. Once she got home, we spoke on the phone, but she became cold as ice to me. She would wait for me to go to work and then call Ken to poison his mind. The year passed swiftly, and I spoke to Bessie only two times.

Something was changing in Ken during this time. He seemed stronger and more confident and talked about his mum less and less. There were many nights I got home from work and he mentioned that she called, but he wasn't planning on calling her back. Little by little, he seemed happier.

I did not think she would ever return, but she called that September and asked to come for a visit. She wanted to come in time to celebrate her February birthday. I thought at the time that she must be crazy. Hadn't we already had a winter nightmare with her the year before? I guess she sensed the fact that Ken was thinking things through and distancing himself from her. She probably thought I was doing it, but it had nothing to do with me. Our guess is that she was losing control and couldn't get her claws into her son from a distance. She felt the urgent need to come back to regain control and perhaps to deliver one last blow, hoping to separate us. I was accommodating toward her because it made my husband happy. He was still in denial somewhat. He was beginning to see the light, but he had a long way to go.

We picked her up at the airport, and she immediately started complaining about the cold weather. Once we got her home, we had to turn up our heat to nearly eighty-five degrees in order for her to feel good. We were walking around with shorts and tank tops, and she was huddled in front of our fireplace with blankets around her and her son at her side asking what he could do for her. This went on day after day.

The day arrived for us to celebrate Bessie's birthday. She was in a fairly good mood when the day started. It was always that way when everything was about her. Later, She was complaining to Ken about being cold, and she was complaining that she had gained weight here and that her jeans were tight. It's not like I had opened her mouth and force-fed her. Besides, she looked good and healthy. Normally, she was quite thin, and we both commented on how good she looked. I just rolled my eyes from the other room, breathed in, breathed out and got on with Bessie's birthday dinner. I had also made her favorite chocolate cake so that we could sing *Happy Birthday*. I wondered briefly if she would even eat the cake after the issue over tight jeans. We had presents, and she opened them and was thankful and grateful for them. Things seemed to be looking up for a good evening.

We all sat down to dinner and in a few moments heard a "bing-bong" coming from my computer. Our network had Skype, which allows people to have web chats via the computer. I had many of Ken's family as contacts on the program and had spoken with them via email and webcam on many occasions. I had made different sounds for different contacts, so I knew who was calling according to the sound. Since this call was coming in with the generic tone, I wasn't sure who it was. I thought it might be a family member calling Mum to extend birthday greetings. I went to the computer and clicked to accept the call. There was a woman on my computer screen approximately forty years old with long hair and a beautiful face but completely shit-faced drunk. She was slurring her words, and her eyelids were droopy. Still, I could detect a British accent and kept hearing the word Mum. I could only assume this was one of Ken's sisters wishing to speak to his Mum. I immediately applied a custom tone to her account. I called to Ken, and he got up from the dinner table to see what I wanted. He saw the girl and confirmed that it was his youngest sister, Pat. Soon, my youngest daughter and Ken's mum got up from the dinner table. I figured we could heat up the food later if we needed to. Once we all got in front of the screen, we found that she was so drunk that she could barely speak. She was slurring her words and not making much sense. Still, I think her birthday wishes came through, so we all sat with her for a few minutes, blew kisses to her, and left the computer to go back to the dinner table.

Within two minutes, my message program sounded again, indicating to me that Pat was back online. I didn't want to interrupt dinner, so instead of accepting the incoming call, I turned down the sound until dinner was over. We finished dinner about twenty minutes later, and I turned the sound back up while bringing dishes into the kitchen. Immediately, I heard Pat's sound ring again. I accepted the call and saw her lying on her side and crying into the webcam. She was begging me for money and a passport and insisted that I send it to her so she could come to America. She wanted to spend the rest of Mum's vacation with her. My head just about burst. I was already overwhelmed with the mother visiting; what was going to happen next? Would Ken buy a ticket for Pat to come over too? Would I then be outnumbered and treated like shit in my own home? This was his family. I would deal with whatever came up, but I would let him decide. I called to Ken in the other room. He looked at Pat on the screen and just sighed. He was tired of this, and his patience was gone. I decided to leave the room and let Ken deal with her. He was trying to reason with her as I headed to the living room, to turn on a film we had all agreed to watch. We were letting dinner settle before we had cake and would sing *Happy Birthday* to Mum after the movie. Ken came back into the living room and settled in next to me, and we started the movie. Five minutes into it, the now-familiar Pat sound came from the computer again. I looked at Ken and shrugged my shoulders, giving him the idea that I wasn't going to do a thing about it. He could decide what to do next. He could simply ignore it, or he could go back to speak to her. There was no way I was getting involved. But at that moment, Bessie started shouting at me. "You will *not* have a go at my Pat. You don't even know it is Pat." I explained to her that since I was a programmer, I was familiar with the computer and did in fact know it was Pat. She stormed upstairs, and everything went from bad to worse—yet again.

I didn't want to reason with her, and I knew she felt the same. However, Ken looked as if he had been through a war. His face showed his pain, and I wanted to alleviate his stress. I told him I would handle it, but I asked him if he trusted me to do so. He basically told me to do anything I could to just finish it off. He didn't want her back here again. I was shocked. He was finally beginning to see that her behavior was not normal. He said his life had been so peaceful until this "circus" began. He was beginning to see the light. I followed Bessie upstairs, knocked on her door, and went in to sit on the bed next to her. I said we seemed to be at an impasse. She seemed to agree. I explained that we must learn to get along or that we could not be together here again.

She got a horrible look on her face that changed her entire demeanor. At that moment, she resembled an old, scary, witch. With venom in her words, she informed me that she hated me and my kids because they were spoiled rotten and she hated America and all Americans. She also knocked down my family, including my mother and brother and his children.

I breathed in, I breathed out, and then I let her have it. Unlike her own children, I faced her with fury and honesty. I wanted no stone left unturned. I said nobody would ever speak ill of my kids, my husband, or my family and that she and I were going to have it out once and for all. I told her that I didn't think we could ever please her and she was upsetting everyone here, especially Ken. I explained that she should do the decent thing and just leave. I also told her that if she hated it here so much that she should never come back. I was not shocked when she agreed. This was probably the only thing we ever saw eye to eye on.

We spent yet more money taking her back to the airport and getting her onto an earlier flight. We all felt the weight of frustration leave as soon as she walked through the gate. She uttered no words, she gave no hugs, and she barely waved to any of us as she went through the airport security gate.

Months went by before we spoke to her again. One final conversation between her and me was still to come. But for now, it was over.

One of Ken's sisters was calling frequently trying to get Ken and me to patch things up with Mum. Aside from that, we spoke to Lena and to Ken's brother Tim only. No words with Bessie at all. These were some of the happiest times in our lives.

One day, Tim shared some issues with Ken and me. Apparently, his son was going down a bad path. He was involved with some bad friends, and he no longer cared for school and basically just stopped going. Ken got on the phone with him and made him an offer. He told him that if he went back to school and got his head screwed on straight, then Ken would treat him to an all-expenses-paid trip to America. We all hung up the phone and felt good about helping Ken's brother in this manner.

Within one hour, that horrible feeling sank into the pit of my stomach again as the phone rang. I answered, and there was Bessie shouting into the phone. She told me that I was causing trouble in the family again and she would not have it. I asked her what she was talking about, and she said it was because we offered a free trip to Tim's son.

I was done. I handed the phone to Ken, and I saw and heard him explode. He let Bessie have it that day, and rightfully so. He let her know in no uncertain terms that she was sick in the head. She enjoyed watching the family divide. She enjoyed that siblings had issues with one another but not with her. She felt entitled to rule Ken's decisions. He told her how she had no right to say who could or could not come to visit. He also told her that his life was on track and suited him well and that she had been responsible for his nervous, unstable state of mind. He also said that whenever he brought his children over when they were younger, she would always just go into the bedroom and pretend she didn't feel well. His opinion was that she didn't like children much. She hung up on him. He was furious. I had never seen him like this. That was the day that Ken finally took control away from his mother and took control of his own life.

Through the remaining year, we fully expected Bessie to call and apologize. She never did. Instead, she wrote a letter telling Ken that his brother Tim was a horrible person and he should not ever have contact with him again. She also said bad things about every one of her other children and basically told Ken that he was the only one she cared about. She mentioned that after she died, Ken would look up into the sky and say, "You were *so* right, Mum. They are all bad, and I should have listened to you."

We were flabbergasted. Ken immediately ripped the letter into a million pieces and shook his head. "She is still trying to control me after all of this, but it will never work again," he said.

During these years, Ken's dad passed away. He had been too sick the entire time I had known Ken to come to the USA for a visit. We did the right thing. and paid for Ken to go back home twice. Once, before his father died in order to spend time with him, and again after his dad died for the funeral. We contributed financially to the family when his dad died. We did it with clean hearts. It gave us closure. Ken told me that he had a chance to engage in a heart-to-heart talk with his dad. He advised Ken to get home to America and stay there and never look back. His dad told him that there was nothing but drama going on constantly within the family and that he should get out while he could. Each time Ken came back from there, he could talk only about what a bundle of nerves he was and that he was grateful to be home. He admitted after one of these trips that he was very happy with his life in America and that it took him a trip or two back home to realize it. Never again would he doubt himself for making the decision to live here. He also decided that he would never again want to deal with his mum. She had one too many bouts of "crazy" to mention, and he could not stand to be around her any longer than necessary. He told me stories about being home with her on his last visit that made my skin crawl, but he felt proud that he had gone home, treated her with respect each time, and never again fought with her. It was pointless. She would never be in our lives again.

Ken's entire family is broken apart. Her divide-and-conquer scenario worked. Bessie is in contact with only two of her five children. We know that we are still a source of conversation for her, but it means nothing to us. She is the type of person who will still be telling the same sad stories and lies until the day she leaves this earth. In my mind, I can still hear her saying over and over, "I'm not a bad penny." But she was the worst.

We had no choice but to get help for ourselves and our little family in the form of counselors and references, including books that were recommended to us. We have now been educated enough to know that Bessie is a full-blown narcissist who simply stopped getting her own way with us. When a narcissist is confronted, he or she simply cuts that person from his or her life and moves on to the next victim(s). We were lucky to get away from her and keep our little family intact. Our relationship with her is over forever.

Although we do not wish her or anyone else harm, it will be a relief for us one day when we hear of her passing. My poor husband and his sisters and brother never had a chance at a normal life. Mothers are supposed to protect children, and instead Bessie just thought about herself and let the worst things happen to them.

I am thankful for my husband and my sister-in-law Lena and her family, and all the kids in Ken's family who got away. Those who remain close to us are always in our hearts and minds. There is no need to speak about any of it anymore because we all have happy, positive lives, and we just want to move forward. We have never been happier since Ken cut out this loser.

The Moral: Blood may be thicker than water. However, when you get a blood clot, it is lethal. Dangerous people may be in your family, but you can and should cut them away from your life because the clot will destroy you.

A NOTE FROM THE AUTHOR

Kyle is not mentioned much in the last few chapters of the book. This is only because he and I have separately moved around this beautiful country with our different relationships, jobs and adventures.

Now that I have a husband and grown children, I tend to bounce ideas and questions off of them first.

To this day, however, Kyle and I remain in touch and I still consider him one of my best friends. I could never have survived the majority of these incidents without his love and support. Thank you Kyle.

www.ingramcontent.com/pod-product-compliance
Lightning Source LLC
Chambersburg PA
CBHW072208090426

42740CB00012B/2435